D1187277

RABELAISIAN DIALECTIC
AND THE PLATONIC-HERMETIC TRADITION

RABELAISIAN DIALECTIC

AND THE
PLATONIC-HERMETIC TRADITION

G. Mallary Masters

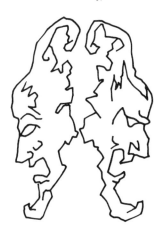

STATE UNIVERSITY OF NEW YORK PRESS
ALBANY

MANUFACTURED IN THE UNITED STATES OF AMERICA
DESIGNER: RHODA C. CURLEY

PREFACE

ince my major concern is with Rabelais's thought as a revelation of his attitude to the Platonic and Hermetic tradition, it is of no consequence whether I personally accept or reject the concept of an ordered universe. Therefore, I have not begun this preface to a study of the "occult" sciences by a disavowal of my own belief in the efficacy of the Hermetic for the twentieth century. But I do request that the reader keep in mind that present distinctions between science and pseudo-science are not always valid for Rabelais and for his time. It will, in fact, be necessary for the modern reader to put aside those distinctions if he wishes to understand Rabelais in his own terms. I have tried, to the degree that it is objectively possible, to use the terminology of the Renaissance in order to clarify the thought of that period for the modern reader. Finally, it goes without saying that neither the approach I have used nor the concepts set forth are exclusively my own, for I am deeply indebted to many of my colleagues and former teachers for their help.

I am very pleased to acknowledge the patient guidance of Professor Nathan Edelman without whose assistance the original dissertation on which this present edition was based could not have been completed. I am grateful to him and to Professor Henry Hornik, from whom more than any others I received my inspiration for studying the Renaissance, for their guidance in methods of literary analysis, and for their constant willingness to listen to and correct, when necessary, my interpretation of the text. To my colleagues Professors Bernard F. Huppé and Anthony L. Pellegrini I give my thanks for their thoughtful advice about the stylistic transformation of this manuscript from dissertation to monograph. For their help in locating texts and critical materials I express my sincere gratitude to the librarians of the Johns Hopkins University Library (especially Mlles. Hubbard and Eisenhardt), of the Library of Congress, the Folger Library, the Peabody Library, the Bibliothèque Nationale, the

Bibliothèque Mazarine, the Bibliothèque de l'Arsenal, and the Library of the University of Missouri (especially Mrs. Ann-Todd Rubey and Miss Lucille M. Cobb).

Financial assistance given by the National Defense Education Act and Woodrow Wilson Foundation permitted me to study without interruption and to begin research in France before completing my dissertation at the Johns Hopkins University. I also wish to thank the Research Administration of the University of Missouri for numerous grants for materials, for typing, for travel, and especially for the Summer Research Grant (1965) that enabled me to consult in France and Switzerland additional texts for the revision of the manuscript. It is self-evident that though I am indebted to those named and unnamed who contributed to the completion of this project, I am responsible for all the errors contained herein.

G. M. M.

The State University of New York
at Binghamton
March, 1968

nless otherwise indicated, all references to the text of Rabelais will be in accordance with the standard critical editions, François Rabelais, *Œuvres,* ed. Abel Lefranc, *et al.,* for the first three books and the first seventeen chapters of the *Quart Livre,* and Rabelais, *Œuvres complètes,* ed. Jean Plattard, for the remaining chapters of the fourth book and the *Cinquiesme Livre.* References will usually be included in parentheses in the text and will consist of chapter numbers in Arabic numerals and the names of the five books abbreviated as follows: *Gargantua, G; Pantagruel, P; Tiers Livre, TL; Quart Livre, QL;* and *Cinquiesme Livre, CL.* The orthography of the critical editions will be used in preference to modern French. In addition to those editions cited, the critical editions of Jacques Boulenger, Rabelais, *Œuvres complètes,* Charles Marty-Laveaux, Rabelais, *Les Œuvres,* and Jean Martin, *Les Œuvres,* will be used when helpful.

References to the Bible will be to the Vulgate edition of the *Biblia Sacra.*

With the exception of unpublished dissertations, all manuscripts will be italicized in bibliographical notations. The following abbreviations will be used:

B.N.   Bibliothèque Nationale
Ms. fr.   Manuscrit français
n. a.   Nouvelle acquisition.

The abbreviations that follow will be used for periodicals and publications in series:

Annales musicolog.	Société de Musique d'autrefois. *Annales musicologiques, moyen-âge et renaissance.*
BBB	*Bulletin du bibliophile et du bibliothécaire.*
BHR	*Bibliothèque d'humanisme et renaissance.*
HR	*Humanisme et renaissance.*
MLN	*Modern Language Notes.*

MLQ	*Modern Language Quarterly.*
MLR	*Modern Language Review.*
PMLA	*Publications of the Modern Language Association of America.*
RCC	*Revue des cours et conférences.*
RER	*Revue des études rabelaisiennes.*
RHLF	*Revue d'histoire littéraire de la France.*
RSS	*Revue du seizième siècle.*
STFM	Société des textes français modernes.

We gratefully acknowledge permission to cite from the following works: Librairie Champion, Rabelais, *Œuvres,* ed. Lefranc, t. I-V; Librairie Droz S.A., Rabelais, *Œuvres,* ed. Lefranc, t. VI, and La Ramée, *Dialectique* (1555), ed. Michel Dassonville; Maison Dunod, François Secret, *Les Kabbalistes chrétiens de la renaissance;* Harper & Row, Publishers, Inc., Eckhart, *Meister Eckhart, A Modern Translation;* M. l'Abbé Raymond Marcel, *Commentaire sur le Banquet de Platon;* Routledge & Kegan Paul Ltd., Johan Huizinga, *Homo Ludens: A Study of the Play-Element in Culture;* and Société d'édition "Les Belles Lettres," Rabelais, *Œuvres complètes,* ed. Plattard.

TABLE OF CONTENTS

RABELAISIAN DIALECTIC
AND THE PLATONIC-HERMETIC TRADITION

abelais's literary work is not a treatise on the philosophy associated with Plato and Hermes Trismegistus, nor does that system of thought or any other exclusively represent Rabelais. But his five books do abound with images like the *boites dites Silenes*[1] that have their basis in the Platonic-Hermetic tradition. Those images and the related allegorical myths of the *Gargantua* and *Pantagruel* reflect, moreover, the dialectic of opposites inherent in Platonism and Hermetism.[2] By way of introduction to this study of Rabelais's work in the perspective of that dialectic, it is appropriate to consider first the general meaning and relationship the philosophies of Plato and the *corpus hermeticum* had for Rabelais and then to look at the dialectic common to both.

The biographical details of Rabelais's interest in Plato have become a familiar aspect of Rabelaisian criticism. For example, one knows of the difficulties he and Pierre Lamy had in studying Plato at Fontenay-le-Comte, their participation while there in the Platonically oriented circle of Tiraqueau and Bouchard, Rabelais's correspondence with the humanist Budé, and his possession of Ficino's editions of Plato and the *Opuscula* of Dionysius the Areopagite.[3] The facts are few but significant, for they suggest not only that Rabelais knew Plato but also that he, along with other Renaissance Platonists, read him as one of the *prisci theologi*.[4]

Rabelais and the Florentines believed that the *prisci* had participated in a partial pre-Christian revelation which began with Adam and which Abraham or Moses transmitted in turn to the Egyptian priests. As Rabelais suggests in the closing chapter of the last book (*CL*/47), Zoroaster, Hermes Trismegistus, the Druids, Orpheus, Pythagoras, and Plato were all thought to have inherited from Egypt the secret wisdom of the *prisca theologia*. Plato as the last of the *prisci* conveyed the tradition to the Academy, which then passed it on to the Alexandrian Neoplatonists. Last in the succession were the Platonizers of the

Middle Ages and Renaissance who also regarded themselves as *Platonici*. Thus, when Rabelais as a Renaissance humanist read Plato, he interpreted him in the light of a long line of "Platonists" who included the immediate followers of Plato, Alexandrians, and Christians. For Rabelais there was no significant distinction in content among any of the Platonists; he did not, therefore, differentiate between a Neoplatonist of the Alexandrian period or one of the Christian era.[5]

If one may speak of a purely secular Platonism of the Christian era, it must be within terms of the Byzantine or Arabic traditions, for the available Latin translations and commentaries of Platonic texts were put to *theological* use. Latin Christian Platonism had its sources in the several stages of Platonism—the Athenian Academy, Hellenistic Middle Platonism, and Alexandrian Neoplatonism. All three currents left direct traces in the theological speculations of both Greek and Latin Patristics, but the high Middle Ages depended almost entirely on Latin fragments of Plato's dialogues, especially Chalcidius' translation of the *Timaeus* and his commentaries; on the pseudo-Platonic treatises of Macrobius, Apuleius, Seneca, and Cicero, among others; and primarily on the writings of Augustine, Boethius, and Dionysius the Areopagite. The Platonic tradition left its major imprint on the Christian conception of the spiritual, nonmaterial nature of man, the idea of cosmological harmony, and, of course, the conception of Being, Unity, and Ideal forms. The "Platonic" tradition of Johannes Scotus Erigena, Saint Anselm of Canterbury, and theologians of the twelfth century was continued, in spite of the predominantly Aristotelian empiricism of Scholasticism, in the speculations of Albert the Great, Roger Bacon, Saint Bonaventure and the Franciscans, and Duns Scotus and his school. Even the "Aristotelian" commentaries of Averroes and Avicenna showed traces of Neoplatonic interpretation. Thus, when they were introduced into the Latin West, they also added to the undercurrent of Platonic influence.[6] It is apparent, therefore, that the doctrines of Platonism were not forgotten in the Middle

Ages, but the medieval speculators were primarily Christian theologians who drew from the Platonists what was useful to them. And although the Renaissance showed a renewed interest in the Platonic texts and chose Plato as the model in metaphysics, the humanists never forgot Aristotle or their Christian heritage.

Unlike the early French Platonists, Rabelais did not personally know the Florentines. But he shared with Fichet (who corresponded with Bessarion and "protected" Pico during his flight to Paris) and with Gaguin (who knew Bessarion and Pico as well as Ficino) their humanistic and theological orientation of Platonism. Similarly, he shared Lefevre's interest in Aristotle, Cusanus, Dionysius the Areopagite, and the mystical Platonism of Saint Augustine, which Lefevre synthesized with the philological emphasis of the early Reform. Like Symphorien Champier, Rabelais showed interest in the cosmological and physiological aspects of Platonic philosophy in their relation to Arabic and Greek medicine and to free will.[7] Similarly, Rabelais, like his contemporaries and predecessors, interpreted Plato in the light of the Hermetic sciences.

In addition to interpreting Plato through the Neoplatonic speculations of some eighteen hundred years, Rabelais related him to the initiatory rites evoked by the name of Orpheus and the occult sciences attributed to Zoroaster and Hermes Trismegistus, namely, astrology, alchemy, and magic.[8] Each of these sciences was thought to be veiled by secrecy, but the name of Hermes became representative of all occult sciences connected with Renaissance Platonism. Thus, Hermetism includes not only the philosophy of the *corpus hermeticum,* but it also encompasses the Cabala; the initiatory cults of Pythagoras, Dionysos, and Orpheus; alchemy; magic; astrology; and Platonism and Neoplatonism. Although a study of Platonism in Rabelais cannot be separated from Hermetism, it is appropriate to follow the differentiation of the terms "Platonism" and "Hermetism" that the Renaissance writers made as a matter of convenience.[9] The relationship of these sciences is further complicated by their association with Christianity. Inasmuch as Renaissance humanists found a philosophical relationship between Christian doctrine and the Platonic-Hermetic tradition, any analysis of that tradition would be incomplete without placing it in the perspective of Christian theology. For the Renaissance sought and found in its own terms an essential unity of thought. It achieved a resolution of theological and philosophical opposites in a synthesis of Judaeo-Christian theology and humanistic philosophy. In that synthesis the thinkers of the period saw a dynamic balance between seemingly dichotomous extremes of a spiritual and philosophical idealism and the material reality of the present.

Rabelais's literary work reflects the dynamic tension of the extremes. His humor, often gross and exaggerated when judged by present tastes, shows a playful, gay acceptance of physical pleasures. In Platonism, on the other hand, he and his age see an expression of their idealism, of an intellectual desire to transcend the elemental world of matter which is subject to flux, change, and transformation through death and rebirth. For Rabelais, man is inconstant; he is incapable of sustained knowledge of himself, of the world, and of the divine. At the same time he is capable of angelic insight and mastery of the natural world through an understanding of its ordered laws. A creature of superstition and *sapience,* of vice and virtue, and of *philautia* and *caritas,* man lives in a temporal universe characterized by extremes as we see in the parallel series: idea and form, intellect and matter, soul and body. But for the man of the Renaissance those extremes are not antithetical. For Rabelais, as for Cusanus, those opposites coincide in the infinity of God who is present everywhere in the world of His creation and who transcends it at the same time.[10] This concept of coincidence is suggested by Bacbuc in the final episode of Book V.

Bacbuc, just before partially enumerating the *prisci,* refers to the concept of the *Dieu caché,* which is basic to both Platonism and Hermetism (*CL*/47).[11] The Egyptians, she says, called the *Dieu souverain* "L'Abscond, le Mussé, le Caché." Her statement obviously pertains to the doctrine of divine transcendence, that is, the belief that God is invisible, indefinable, and incomprehensible to man. Man can at best attain a partial knowledge of God through negative theology by indicating what God is not. On the positive side, the best expression of divine nature remains a metaphor: "ceste sphere intellectuelle de laquelle en tous lieux est le centre et n'a en lieu aucun circonference, que nous appelons Dieu." Rabelais attributes this image of the sphere, as reiterated by Bacbuc, to Hermes, but he probably borrowed it from Cusanus or the Scholastics.[12] It combines both the immanence and transcendence of the divine, for while it does not limit the divine essence, it suggests that God is present everywhere in creation.

Rabelais's universe is ordered and harmonic, for it is an imitation of the world of divine Ideas. But it is simultaneously subject to the constant transformation of the elements. For him truth dependent on empirical experience and intuitive reason is partial. Man is both body and soul, matter and intellect, animal and angel. He is neither one nor the other exclusively, but a dynamic combination of the two. Similarly, for him truth consists in neither of the extremes but in both even as it transcends and includes them both. Thus the world of time and the eternal are reconciled, and Rabelais finds a meaningful relationship for them in a philosophical dialectic that reflects the unity of his thought. The themes of the Platonic-Hermetic tradition examined in this study mirror such a unity.

For Ficino, Pico, and Rabelais, man is at the center of the hierarchical scale of being.[13] A composite of matter and intellect, he possesses through reason the *means* of resolving the opposing elements of his nature. By this they did not mean that man is reason and nothing more. Reason, or logic, is rather a dynamic relationship between angelic intellect and bestial passion, between intuitive knowledge and empirical fact. Or, as Pascal has so succinctly phrased it, "qui veut faire l'ange fait la bête." [14] Man, who has the potentiality of angel and animal, is not and can not be exclusively one or the other. Through logic and reasonable

control, however, he partakes of both. And on the scale of the
little world of man he reenacts the cosmic dynamism embodied in
the humanity of Christ.

For Rabelais, as for Cusanus, the humanness of Christ is the
aspect of the Godhead most often cited. The Augustinian term
Servateur, which Rabelais employs most often in referring to the
divinity, emphasizes in the Platonically oriented triad of *Createur*
(Beginning), *Servateur* (Middle) and *Conservateur* (End),
Christ as Healer and Redeemer (*QL/65*). These are the essential
qualities of the humanity of Christ whom Rabelais also philosophically identifies with Pan, stating through Pantagruel that
Pan and Christ are one (*QL/28*). In this context, Christ as Pan,
the Platonic All, is another manifestation of God.[15] Through his
human form He resolves the dichotomy of the transcendent-
immanent Creator. As Logos become flesh (*Verbum incarnatum*),
He bridges the gap between God and microcosm, between God
and macrocosm and between microcosm and macrocosm. For He
is all, above and in all. Similarly, man as a creature of logic
bridges the gap between oneness and multiplicity. Through
reason he establishes himself in the dynamic relationship between
idea and form, Creator and creation, and God and Nature—a
relationship basic to the Platonic-Hermetic dialectic.

When examined in the light of a single philosophical tradition
basic to it and expressed through it, the literary work of Rabelais
shows a fundamental unity. In the process of this examination, a
secondary conclusion or hypothesis presents itself, that is, the
authenticity of the fifth book. But the thesis of authenticity is
subordinate to the investigation of the Platonic-Hermetic tradition. The reader of this study is therefore invited initially to as-
sume the authenticity of Book V and then finally, in appendix,
to review the evidence in the light of the demonstrated dialectical
unity.

Although the dialectic of coincidence of opposites is inherent
in Rabelais's way of thinking and his *Weltanschauung* as reflected in his literary work, the latter does not constitute a

speculative treatise. Nevertheless, it does illustrate that dialectic by the literary means of image, symbol, myth, and allegory. The oneness of the Platonic-Hermetic tradition is patently beyond dispute, but to facilitate dealing with the several aspects of that tradition, the meaning of Platonism and Hermetism in Rabelais will be examined separately. Although this procedure will necessarily entail occasional repetition of references to certain episodes, it will lead to a clearer understanding of the two extremes of Rabelais's dialectic: Platonic idealism vs. Hermetic naturalism, or intuitive reason vs. empiricism. Such an investigation of naturalism also points to the complementary character of Aristotelian empiricism and Platonic intuition and of Epicurean "materialism" and Platonic *voluptas*. Finally, in order to understand the dual series of extremes, it has been necessary to consider the role of logic as a bridge between them just as the chapter on *"Homo bibens"* provides a logical link between the chapters on "Rabelais *platonicus"* and "Rabelais *hermeticus."*

NOTES

1. François Rabelais, "Prologue," *Gargantua, Œuvres,* ed. Abel Lefranc, *et al.* I, 3–18. Further references will be to this standard critical edition of Rabelais's work where possible. Other critical editions cited and abbreviations used throughout this study are given in "A Bibliographical Note," pp. ix–xi.

2. The term *dialectic,* as used in this study, has three meanings: (1) in general, *dialogue,* in the philosophical sense; (2) *a mode of thought* or, as Pierre de La Ramée has defined it in his *Dialectique,* ed. Michel Dassonville, p. 61, "l'art de bien raisonner;" (3) a *means to knowledge,* especially intuitive knowledge. The dialectic of the coincidence of opposites, which subsumes all three meanings, is basic to the thought of Nicholas Cusanus. His treatises *De docta ignorantia* and *Idiota* were published in his *Opera.* See also Ernst Cassirer, *The Individual and the Cosmos in Renaissance Philosophy,* trans. Mario Domandi, pp. 7–45, and *Das Erkenntnisproblem in der Philosophie und Wissenschaft der neuren Zeit,* I, 21–61; and Vincent Martin, "The Dialectical Process in the Philosophy of Nicholas of Cusa," *Laval théologique et philosophique,* V (1949), 213–68. Charles de Bouelles (Carolus Bovillus), who adapted Cusanus' dialectic in an Aristotelian framework, emphasized the importance of reason in bridging the gap between the One and the many in his treatise *De sapiente* (1509), in Ernst Cassirer, *Individuum und Kosmos in der Philosophie der Renaissance,* pp. 299–412. See also Cassirer, *Individual and the Cosmos,* pp. 88–93, and *Erkenntnisproblem,* I, 62–72.

3. For a discussion of Rabelaisian Platonism, see Abel Lefranc, "Le Platon de Rabelais," *BBB* (1901), 105–14, 169–81; Robert Marichal, "L'Attitude de Rabelais devant le néoplatonisme et l'italianisme (*Quart Livre,* Ch. ix à xi)," in *François Rabelais: Ouvrage publié pour le quatrième centenaire de sa mort,* pp. 181–84; G. Mallary Masters, "The Hermetic and Platonic Traditions in Rabelais' Dive Bouteille," *Studi Francesi,* X (1966), 15–29; and, for a more complete summary of Platonic details, my unpublished doctoral dissertation "The Platonic and Hermetic Tradition and the *Cinquiesme Livre* of François Rabelais" (The Johns Hopkins University, 1964). For the correspondence with Budé, see Louis Delaruelle, *Répertoire analytique et chronologique de la correspondance de Guillaume Budé,* pp. 140–41, 197–200. The texts of the letters are found in Rabelais, *Œuvres,* ed. Marty-Laveaux, III, 289–98. For the influence of the circle of Tiraqueau, see Rabelais, ed. Plattard, V, 187;

Rabelais, ed. Boulenger, n. 1, p. 917; J. Barat, "L'Influence de Tiraqueau sur Rabelais," *RER*, II (1905), 138–55, 253–75; and Lefranc, "Etude sur le *Tiers Livre*" in Rabelais, *Tiers Livre*, t. V, xxxix–lx.

4. See Walter Mönch, *Die italienische Platonrenaissance und ihre Bedeutung für Frankreichs Literatur und Geistesgeschichte (1450–1550)*, pp. 3–12.

5. André Chastel, *Marsile Ficin et l'art*, pp. 39–46; P. O. Kristeller, *The Philosophy of Marsilio Ficino*, trans. Virginia Conant, pp. 10–29. The fact that Rabelais and other Renaissance humanists interpreted Plato through Alexandrian and Christian Platonists has an immediate significance for any investigation of Renaissance Platonism, in that one does not always have to show a direct reading of Plato. Rabelais knew Plato and the several stages of Platonism as well.

6. The Arabic, Byzantine, and Latin traditions of Platonism are sketched by Raymond Klibansky, *The Continuity of the Platonic Tradition during the Middle Ages*. The influence of Platonic thought on the Latin Middle Ages is discussed by Paul Shorey, *Platonism, Ancient and Modern*, pp. 62–117, and Etienne Gilson, *History of Christian Philosophy in the Middle Ages*, among others. The Platonic undercurrent of the late Middle Ages and the Renaissance attitude toward Augustine is set forth by P. O. Kristeller, "Augustine and the Renaissance," *International Science*, I (1941), 7–14.

7. Mönch, *Die italienische Platonrenaissance*, pp. 184–203, 212–300; A.-J. Festugière, *La Philosophie de l'amour de Marsile Ficin et son influence sur la littérature française au XVIe siècle*, pp. 67–78.

8. D. P. Walker, "Orpheus the Theologian and Renaissance Platonists," *Journal of the Warburg and Courtauld Institutes*, XVI (1953), 100–120.

9. For clarity the term "Platonism" will be used to include the philosophical thought of Plato and the Alexandrian Neoplatonists as well as the Neoplatonists of the Middle Ages and of the Renaissance, whereas "Hermetism," in general, will designate the sciences of astrology, alchemy, magic, the cabala, and the initiatory cults. For a discussion of the historical and philosophical relationship of Hermetism to the occult sciences, cf. A.-J. Festugière, *La Révélation d'Hermès Trismégiste*, I, 89–308.

10. Cassirer, *Individual and the Cosmos*, pp. 38–45.

11. The Hermetic doctrines of God as revealed in the Cosmos (*le Dieu caché*) and the transcendence of God (*le Dieu inconnu*) are discussed by Festugière, *La Révélation*, respectively, in Vols. II and IV.

12. See also *TL,* Ch. 13, for a similar example of the image. For possible Scholastic sources, see A. J. Krailsheimer, *Rabelais and the Franciscans,* pp. 98–99. For a sketch of the history of the image, see Abel Lefranc, *Grands écrivains français de la renaissance,* especially pp. 174–85, who cites examples from Empedocles, Plato, Plotinus, Vincent of Beauvais, Bonaventura, Cusanus, Ficino, Marguerite de Navarre, and Pascal, among others. See also Hiram Haydn, *The Counter-Renaissance,* pp. 335–36.

13. Kristeller, *Philosophy of Marsilio Ficino,* pp. 74–91.

14. Blaise Pascal, *Pensées,* ed. Léon Brunschvicg, No. 358, p. 493. See also No. 140, pp. 396–97.

15. Krailsheimer, *Rabelais,* pp. 125–43, discusses the possible sources and the significance of the Pan legend, and gives a numerical tabulation of the Divine Names used by Rabelais, pp. 97–106.

 CHAPTER I: Rabelais Platonicus

abelais shares with Plato a profound sense of play. Their images play on appearance and reality. Their allegorical myths embody a sense of playfulness and arise from the dialectic of opposites that is grounded in a cosmic tension between intellect and matter. Thus Rabelais's conception of literature is Platonic in its orientation. His myths depend, moreover, upon the Platonic-Hermetic tradition for their fullest meaning. The dialectic of that tradition gives both form and content to his literary work.

A study of Rabelais's conception of imagery and allegory in the perspective of the Platonic dialectic serves as an appropriate point of departure for the present analysis. That investigation in turn leads to a review of the myth of the Androgyna and the concept of world harmony that it represents for Rabelais. The first chapter concludes with an examination of the philosophy symbolized by the *pantagruelion,* a philosophy of play and spiritual *voluptas* that Rabelais sets forth in the myth of Pantagruel.

1. PLATONIC IMAGERY: ALLEGORY, MYTH, AND SYMBOL

The images of the *boites dites Silenes* and the *os medulaire* of the "Prologue" to *Gargantua,* like the others to be studied in this chapter, reflect the Platonic tradition in form and content. Both metaphors suggest a play on appearance and reality which is grounded in the dialectic of the coincidence of opposites. They point to the use of allegorical symbolism which is at once a means of hiding truth through hermetic imagery and a way of clarifying truth through allegorical interpretation.

Rabelais, perhaps following Erasmus, makes in the first of these images an analogy between the apothecary boxes and the Socrates that Alcibiades describes in the *Symposium.*[1] In seeming contradiction to their external appearance the *Silenes,* which are covered with grotesque figures from mythology and popular medieval folklore, contain precious drugs.[2] Similarly, Socrates has the appearance of an ugly, drunken lecher, while he actually portrays all the virtues of spiritual beauty. Through the philosophical pursuit of wisdom he embodies all the characteristics of the daimon Love. But Socrates is more than a contemplative philosopher; he is also a teacher. Just as his physical appearance hides moral beauty, so the simplicity and naiveté of his words conceal their intrinsic truth. His metaphors and images, while literally nonsensical, veil true sagacity when they are symbolically interpreted. So Rabelais in explaining his analogy thus points to the need for deciphering his own work.

Having suggested to his reader that he must not stop at the literal level but go on to seek higher meaning, Rabelais adds to the example given by his first metaphor a second, namely the *os medulaire.* Now he compares his reader to Plato's philosophical dog. The dog does not content himself with a facile enjoyment of a bone *per se.* He diligently works at it until he breaks it open, and, thereby, sucks out *la sustantificque mouelle.* So Rabelais's reader may fully hope to find philosophical, political, and social truths hidden under the surface of simple amusing stories. Thus, Rabelais through his two Phythagorean symbols, as he calls the images, clearly places his work in the tradition of allegorical symbolism.

Etienne Gilson has shown that Rabelais's images recall medieval threefold interpretation with allegorical, anagogical, and tropological levels.[3] Based on Augustine's conception of sense and sentence, the figural and literal levels of both scriptural and secular works, the use of allegory was of prime importance for Renaissance humanists.[4] Poets such as Marot employ the traditional metaphors. Politian and Pico relate Biblical, Pythagorean, and Platonic fables to the *prisca theologia.*[5] And Hebreo points to the hermetic use of metaphor within that tradition to conceal the truth of philosophical mysteries from the uninitiated.[6] But, as Rabelais himself suggests, Renaissance humanists diverged from medieval allegory in matters of mythology.

In his study *The Survival of the Pagan Gods* Jean Seznec has shown that there was a growing tendency in the Middle Ages to accept ancient mythology and reinterpret it in terms of Christian doctrine.[7] That this tendency toward a moralizing interpretation continued into the Renaissance can not be doubted; but, as Rabelais demonstrates, its use was not entirely the same. When he questions whether Homer really expressed in his epic poems the allegorical meanings found by glossers from Plutarch to Politian, it is not because he questions method so much as application. Unlike Augustine and the medieval allegorists who found in classical myth prefigurations of Christian dogma, Rabelais and Renaissance humanists insisted upon considering a work in its own light. For example, the Florentine Platonists sought to find the intrinsic meaning of the gods, who represented for them the several virtues. The humanists consequently returned to Homer and to Plato, Aristotle, and other primarily Platonic sources of antiquity, such as Apuleius, to find descriptions of the essential qualities of mythical gods. Similarly, in spite of suggestions to the contrary, as an examination of the *Traité de poesie* of Jehan Thenaud shows, they still consulted medieval compendia and moralizing tracts.[8] In doing so, Renaissance humanists sought moral truth in allegory; they did not look for prefigurations of Christianity. Thus, Rabelais's questioning of the Homeric glosses confirms his earlier statements about sense and sentence and does not deny the need for cracking the bone.[9]

Rabelais equivocally propounds, however, in the "Prologue" a contradictory view about allegory. Most of his introductory comments are about higher interpretation, but toward the end of the "Prologue" he suddenly seems to take an opposite stand. He says his reader need look no further than the surface of his *joyeuses chroniques*. If that statement were taken literally it would deny the validity of the rest of the "Prologue." Perhaps, as Tetel suggests, Rabelais is playing with his readers.[10] Or, more meaningfully, perhaps Rabelais is inviting his reader to play *with* him. Although the significance of play by reference to dialectic and allegory will not be discussed fully until later in this chapter, it should be evident that there is a kind of play behind allegory. Rabelais is now merely extending that play and the allegory itself. His denial of the need to decipher his work literally belies everything he has said. But in the context of the "Prologue" and Rabelais's work as a whole it is a veiled, though negative, confirmation of his comments on allegory. As an attempt at distracting the reader, the statement actually confirms his endeavor to extract the *sustantificque mouelle*. As an example of a play on appearance and reality Rabelais's denial is similar to the many other images and myths of his five books which share a common grounding in the Platonic dialectic.

The Androgyna, the image Rabelais chooses for Gargantua (*G*/8); the *pantagruelion,* which embodies *pantagruélisme* and the ideals of Pantagruel (*TL*/49–52); the *febves en gosses* (*CL*/Prol.); and the mathematical stairway (*CL*/36) and the mystical fountain of Bacbuc's temple (*CL*/41–42) all play on appearance and reality.[11] All are images of sense and sentence. They not only signify an idea by their form but they also embody it, much as the allegorical painting of Platonic Ideas purchased by Pantagruel at Medamothi (*QL*/2) concretely portrays the realm of absolute intellect.[12] The images of Renaissance plastic art as well as those of Rabelais's literary text fulfill the requirements he establishes for hieroglyphic images.

The discussion of hieroglyphs grows out of the context of Rabelais's selecting the Androgyna for Gargantua's image and the related colors blue and white for his livery. Together those colors symbolize *joye celeste*. In assigning them their values Rabelais follows the ancient Egyptian sages who gave meaning to the hieroglyphs; he draws on tradition and not opinion.[13] Unlike the author of the *Blason des couleurs,* who relied on his own arbitrary choice, Rabelais selects his symbols because they contain "la vertu, proprieté et nature" of the subject they represent. Rabelais rejects the usage of courtiers who choose their images, colors, and devices by means of external similarities that puns or plays on words suggest to them. For him an essential relationship must exist between a symbol and whatever it represents. That relationship must be founded on reason, and it must be as logical as the link between a word and the idea it conveys (*G*/9–10).

Rabelais associates words with the Platonic Ideas and essential forms in the episode of the *parolles gelées* (*QL*/55–56). For him as for the Plato of the *Cratylus* and the *Timaeus* the *parolle* should express the idea represented by the object.[14] In a sense the word also embodies the idea, the essential form of the thing it represents. But the word too becomes a "visible" image. Rabelais's metaphorical frozen words melt and thereby reveal their meaning. So we must transcend the external level of words to arrive at their essential value. Thus, the word for Rabelais is more than an Augustinian signifier. Like the hieroglyph, the number, the pictorial image, and the poetical symbol, the word plays on appearance and reality.

All Rabelaisian images play on appearance and reality. They embody a dynamic relationship between external form and intrinsic meaning. They at once express the dialectic of opposites and they are that dialectic. The extremes of the apparent and the real suggest the series of dichotomies of the Platonic-Hermetic dualism. But, at the same time, the images also signify something else—they point beyond the apparent to an idea. They embody the essence of whatever they represent and thereby convey a truth. Because of the gulf between man and the realm of pure intellect, the image is in fact the most certain human expression of truth. Man can not be sure of empirical knowledge, of abstractions arrived at through discursive reason, or of momentary intuitive visions. Since logic is an uncertain expression of truth, man uses the image. The image is a surer means of portraying truth; it is a dialectical link between external form and essential form. It portrays the reasonable order of logic just as the myth of the Androgyna embodies the universal harmony of love.

2. THE ANDROGYNA: THE MYTH OF WORLD HARMONY AND *CARITAS*

Rabelais pointedly associates the Androgyna, the image he chooses for Gargantua to wear, with Christian *caritas*. For the device which accompanies the emblematic figure is the Pauline versicle, ΑΓΑΠΗ ΟΥ ΖΗΤΕΙ ΤΑ ΕΑΥΤΗΣ (*Caritas . . . non quaerit quae sua sunt*).[15] Rabelais's juxtaposition of pagan symbol and Christian concept is, however, not new. He, like Ficino and other Renaissance Platonists, follows Augustine's adaptation of Plato's conception of love and harmony in a setting of Christian theological speculation. In Rabelais, as in Plato's *Symposium* and in Hebreo's *Dialoghi d'amore,* the Androgyna is a symbol of the completeness of man.[16] Man in his prime state was a contemplative creature at one with himself, with nature, and with God. But after man introduced into his life the disorderliness of sin and disobedience, he divided his oneness and was thereafter destined to seek continually his other half. His state of unity before the Fall reflects the Platonic ideal of microcosmic order and universal harmony.

Rabelais symbolizes the concept of cosmological harmony through the images of the mathematical stairway and the astronomical fountain in the episode of the Dive Bouteille. Both are reminders of the *Timaeus* in which Plato metaphorically describes cosmological order in terms of mathematical symbols.[17] Rabelais, following Plato, bases the numbers of the stairway to the Temple de la Dive Bouteille on the "great tetraktys" of Pythagoras:[18]

$$
\begin{array}{cc}
8 & 27 \\
4 & 9 \\
2 & 3 \\
& 1
\end{array}
$$

As Rabelais points out, the sum of the two tetrads (the unity, of course, counted only once) is "54" or one-half of "108," the total number of steps. But this descriptive detail is of extrinsic value within itself. It is of prime interest because it embodies the seven numbers that, in turn, establish the series of means of the musical scale and the seven planetary spheres. The music of the spheres in Plato's myth of Er symbolizes the harmony of the octave as well as the ordered pattern of creation. For Plato that order mirrors the Ideal world of pure intellect.[19] Similarly, Rabelais applies the principle of harmony to cosmological order in associating Orphic music with the planetary fountain. Since the astrological structure of the fountain is to be the subject of another chapter, let it suffice to see in that symbolism a pattern of order similar to Plato's myth of Er. Just as Plato considers *harmony* the principle of *concord* in music, *order* in the macrocosm, *love* in human relationships, *justice* in society, and *reason* in the microcosm, so Rabelais sees a parallelism between macrocosm, microcosm, and state in terms of moderation, harmony, and reasonable order. For him the Androgyna symbolizes the harmony natural to prime man who was created in imitation of cosmological order. Rabelais therefore chooses the Androgyna to embody the ideals represented by Gargantua.

The image of the Androgyna, as has been seen, plays on appearance and reality and thereby demonstrates the extremes of the Platonic dialetic. Similarly, the myth of Gargantua, which embodies in extension the Rabelaisian *caritas* of the Androgyna, is a rhetorical exposition of the dialectical extremes. Through antithesis Rabelais establishes the ideals of Gargantuan education and, then, the ideal of behavior for a philosopher-prince.

Rabelais's reader is certainly aware of the antithetical nature of the early chapters on education (*G*/14–24). The meaningless education of sophistry is contrasted with the "new" Renaissance learning. Under the sophist Maistre Thubal Holoferne and later under the old system at Paris, Gargantua exercises his memory but not his intellect or body. In spite of his attending mass incessantly his spirit is no better. The meaningless repetition of dull grammar and commentaries leaves him as much a stupid, dull, dreamy fool as any barbaric dolt of the Gothic age of shadows. But, in sharp contrast, under his new pedagogue Ponocrates he trains body, mind, and spirit. He uses every minute of his day gainfully. His "new" education teaches him, in the manner of the *Republic,* through humanistic languages and letters and the sciences of the trivium, to think for himself.[20] His scientific curiosity is stimulated by empirical observation of craftsmen and tradesmen at work and by a first hand study of astronomy and natural philosophy. Thus, through rhetorical antitheses Rabelais depicts an ideal of education diametrically opposed to the chaotic state of mind of sophistry. He then uses the episode of the Picrocholine war to establish ideal behavior for a philosopher-prince.

The Picrocholine war is one of the best examples of Rabelais's use of rhetorical extremes. The antithetical behavior of Grandgousier and Gargantua on the one hand and of Picrochole and his followers on the other delineates sharply the respective differences between reason and intellectual chaos. Picrochole is unreasonable. As Grandgousier points out, *l'esprit calumniateur* has seized him (*G*/32). Having abandoned faith, law, reason, humanity, and fear of God (*G*/31), from which the other guiding principles stem, he attacks the lands and peoples of Grandgousier without weighing fully the situation (*G*/28). Picrochole's extreme, uncontrolled anger precipitates his actions, and, as might be expected, his ire is reflected in the advice of his most trusted counselors. In Machiavellian fashion, they spur their prince on to dreams of world conquest (*G*/33). Similarly, Picrochole's men mirror the uncurbed materialistic appetites of their master. His soldiers are supersititious and cowardly. They attack without plan, and they destroy without thought everything before them (*G*/35). Taking into account their chaotic behavior, one is not surprised that the Picrocholines should fall before the calmly organized, orderly, and highly effective defense of their superior adversaries, Grandgousier and Gargantua (*G*/48).

Grandgousier is loath to undertake war. He sends ambassadors to Picrochole ($G/30$–31). He tries to make restitution for the cakes taken forcibly by his men ($G/32$). But, when all his efforts at making peace are thwarted, he resorts to defensive war to protect his people. His behavior and that of Gargantua, whom he summons from Paris, embody the principle of *caritas*. Reason and moderation guide them as they set about to defeat the Picrocholines. Generosity and equanimity determine the peace they effect. Gargantua, who arranges the terms of surrender, forgives all those who have followed Picrochole and provides them with money and food to return home ($G/50$). Picrochole's plans for establishing a global tyranny have ended in befitting ignominy. Robbed and beaten, dressed in peasant rags, he makes his way to Lyons where, ironically, he ekes out the pittance on which his last days depend ($G/49$). Thus, what he had planned as a monument to himself becomes a token of honor and charity for Gargantua and his father. To commemorate their victory Rabelais has Gargantua construct Theleme.

The abbaye de Theleme symbolizes the ideals of Gargantua's Androgyna. Just as Rabelais utilizes rhetorical extremes to contrast the chaos of sophistry and the Picrocholine mentality with the "new" Renaissance education founded in reason, moderation, and charity, so he establishes Theleme in antithesis. The negative side is characterized by the old monastic order that led to lethargic inactivity and by the ecclesiastical hierarchy of bigots and hypocrites whom Rabelais excludes from Theleme. The new order is more an educational Utopia than a monastery. It puts forth an ideal society where young men and women study and play together in harmony. Guided by the principle of intrinsic honor they act with common will. Their actions represent the reason, order, and moderation typical of the *Courtier,* which undoubtedly inspired Rabelais's conception of *caritas*.[21]

Caritas sharply contrasts with the behavioral modes Rabelais sets in opposition to it. Hypocrisy, malevolence, and sophistry give way to reason. The ideal of the philosopher-prince Gargantua replaces the bigotry and superstition of a feudal order.

The harmony and moderation of the individual who represents *caritas* are also realized in the state he directs. Behind the law of the state, behind the reasonable control of the individual, stands the divine intellectual order which they both mirror. For Rabelais the Androgyna is an image of that order, and the *caritas* that the image portrays is both a reflection of divine order and a dialectical means of attaining it. *Caritas* is not only concord on the human scale, but also a dialogical link between man and God. The symbol of the *pantagruelion* and the myth of Pantagruel illustrate that aspect of *caritas*.

3. *PANTAGRUELION: VOLUPTAS,* THE IDEAL OF *HOMO LUDENS*

Appearing at the end of the *Tiers Livre,* the *pantagruelion* links the first three books to the voyage theme of the last two. It represents the wisdom of the sage Pantagruel and symbolizes the quest for self-knowledge. The chapters dedicated to the description of the *pantagruelion* give, in the tradition of Renaissance writers, an encyclopedic sketch of botany and herbal lore. Rabelais carefully develops the external characteristics of the herb through a detailed description of its various parts and its size. He tells how and when it should be prepared. He then enumerates the several methods known for naming plants in antiquity. For example, some were named for their discoverer, as *mercuriale* for Mercury. Others retain the names of their native regions, and still others designate the powers or effects they have. Then, turning again to the *pantagruelion,* Rabelais shows that these ancient methods of naming plants are precedents for giving it the name of Pantagruel.

The *pantagruelion* is similar to its namesake in exterior size and in intrinsic "vertus et singularitez:"

> car, comme Pantagruel a esté l'Idée et exemplaire de toute joyeuse perfection . . . , aussi en Pantagruelion je recon-

gnoys tant de vertus, tant d'energie, tant de perfection, tant
d'effectz admirables . . . . (*TL*/51).

There is, then, a double symbolism present. Pantagruel as "Idée et
exemplaire de toute joyeuse perfection" allegorically incorporates
the "joye celeste" and *caritas* of Gargantua. The *pantagruelion,*
in turn, is a symbolic image or manifestation of Pantagruel,
certainly not in external appearance, but in its intrinsic virtue.
It not only has great medicinal value, but, as hemp from which
rope is made, it also serves as a means to the navigational discover-
ies of new lands and to knowledge. An agent for milling flour
for bread, it equally provides a source of spiritual food: "Icelle
herbe moyenante, les substances invisibles visiblement sont
arrestées, prinses, detenues et comme en prison mises . . . ." Like
flax and hemp in appearance, this herb is also similar to asbestos.
Neither it nor the truth it represents can be destroyed by fire
(*TL*/49–52). Just as the Androgyna portrays spiritual being, so
the *pantagruelion* symbolizes *pantagruélisme,* characterized as a
"certaine gayeté d'esprit conficte en mespris des choses fortuites"
(*QL*/Prol.). But the full significance of the *pantagruelion* can
not be understood without an analysis of that paradoxical
philosophy of which it is the symbol.

The two aspects of the definition obviously contradict one
another. "Gayeté d'esprit" is *apparently* not compatible with
"mespris des choses fortuites." If understood in its most Stoic
form the "mespris" would suggest absolute asceticism and a
complete denial of the gifts of the world. Such an interpretation
contradicts, however, the spirit of Rabelais; we must, therefore,
reject it. Similarly, an examination of Panurge's role in the *Tiers
Livre* will equally invalidate the popular conception of Rabelais's
hedonism.

Through antithesis, Rabelais opposes in Book III the idealism
of the sage Pantagruel to the materialistic attitudes of Panurge.
The latter retains from Book II his characteristic wit and playfulness, which he applies through clever logic to an inversion of cosmological harmony. Panurge's eulogy of debts and debtors

($TL/2-4$) might appear, as Marichal has suggested, to satirize the Ficinian commentaries of Platonic love.[22] Within itself, the eulogy is indeed a parody. But, when the eulogy is placed in total context, it becomes evident that Rabelais conceived Panurge's praise of debts as an ironic inversion of the harmony of the world.

In order to defend his erratic and irresponsible financial management, Panurge initially describes the macrocosm without the mutual interdependence of the planets. If the chain of borrowing between Jupiter and Saturn should be broken, the entire structured cosmos would fall apart. Without a system of celestial credits and debits Venus would lose her influence and veneration, the moon would remain clouded, and the sun would no longer shine with benevolent regard on the earth. The stars, in brief, would no longer have any good influence. The very elements composing all living things would cease their balance. Time itself would stop its regular movements. The world would become a place of discord filled with men become monsters, morally depraved and physically hideous. The microcosm, described in parallel to the astrological structure, would become "un terrible tintamarre." There would be no cooperative interdependence of the various organs and members of the body. The head would no longer lend sight to guide the movement of the feet. The heart would not supply blood for the other organs, and they in turn could not function. The brain would fall into revery, ceasing to cause nervous sensation and muscular movement. But, restore debts, and one could contemplate universal harmony in full effect ($TL/3-4$).

Panurge's use of Platonic language is complex. First, he recognizes the order and harmony of the universe and expresses it through the traditional imagery of the divine philosopher. Panurge similarly sees the continued need for that order in the celestial and elementary worlds as well as individually and socially in the "petit monde." But, in spite of his understanding the need for world harmony, he inverts the principle of divine intellect and *caritas*. He replaces love by a system of debts and credits. Although the harmony-love of Plato and Ficino can be glimpsed through the materialism of Panurge's eulogy, his praise of debts essentially inverts that conception. His characterization contrasts strongly with that of Pantagruel.

Pantagruel interprets Panurge's clever inversion as a sign of wit, but he condemns the practice of debts as folly and madness (*TL*/2). The prince, though amused by his jester's arguments, counters with the sound spiritual counsel of Saint Paul: "Rien (dict le sainct Envoyé) à personne ne doibvez fors amour et dilection mutuelle." Loans should be made only to those who have not gained through their own labor. He charitably forgets the past, putting aside Panurge's debts. But Panurge is obstinate. He still wants to retain them *pro forma* by repaying only the interest. Pantagruel has not persuaded him by reasonable arguments, whether practical, moral, or theological. Now Pantagruel must apply his princely prerogative and duty by firmly and authoritatively putting an end to the debate.

Pantagruel's advice shows a basic polarity between concern for wealth and disdain for it. A certain resolution of the seeming paradox appears in the development of his counsel. One might argue that he chose to reason with Panurge on a level he understood and, therefore, began with a positive consideration of wealth. But such an argument is faulty; it can not logically follow from Rabelais's ideal characterization of the young giant. His arguments rather indicate a duality that depends on the philosophical dialectic of extremes. For just as the symbol is related to the ideal through its incorporation of it, so the physical embodies the spiritual. The extremes of body and soul are not dichotomies. Man, who stands at the mid-point between God and creation, man who contains both the superior Ideas and the lower world of matter, man who reflects the redeeming Humanity of Christ, recreates the world. He thereby effects its salvation and a coincidence of dialectic opposites. The world and body, therefore, take on new meaning. They are no longer bad in themselves.

Though they remain separate from their extremes, they participate with them in the new Renaissance conception of salvation.[23]

Thus the "mespris des choses fortuites" does not imply disdain for worldly things but rather a moderate Stoical attitude toward them and not an absolute indifference to them. Riches, for example, are not bad in themselves. Like other aspects of the world they have their value. Hence for Pantagruel they can be good. He does not give them his whole attention but accepts them in their proper perspective. Panurge, on the other hand, in giving free rein to his sensual appetite is guilty not of avarice, but of the sin associated with it, prodigality.[24] Through intemperance, he inverts the cardinal virtues, replacing their spiritual value with materialism. Instead of the theological virtues he would make credit and hope of repayment, not "Foy et Esperance," the foundation for relations among men. For him, *caritas* is not mutual love, but prodigious giving and riotous indulgence of the senses. Panurge perverts the divine harmony and order of the universe by substituting a system of credits and debits based on usury. For, as Panurge says, usury attempts to create something from nothing. It is equally clear that for Rabelais usury inverts the order of social industry. He does not condemn charitable lending and borrowing when individual effort fails; but usury for him is a corruption, and a social structure built on it is chaotic and intemperate.[25] Intemperance or chaos, in the context of world harmony, results from the dominance of the sensual appetite over reason. That dominance suggests in turn the antithesis of *voluptas* and bestiality, the latter represented by Gaster.

Rabelais portrays Messer Gaster, not Love, as the first "maistre es arts de ce monde."[26] He tyrannically demands and receives honor and obedience from the whole world; the respect shown him is so considerable that he passes before kings, emperors, and even the Pope. Gaster listens to no one. His gestures indicate his obduracy, his physical directness, and his inability to communicate on the intellectual plane. Everyone obeys his slightest whim and labors to serve him. In recompense he has invented "toutes ars, toutes machines, tous metiers, tous engins et subtilitez." But he does not limit his arts and influence to human society. In a litany resounding with the satirical phrase, "et tout pour la trippe!", Rabelais enumerates the ways in which Gaster tames the brutes, bending them also to his will.

The enumeration presents an excellent example of the ironic progression of which Rabelais is a literary master. He begins with those birds such as ravens and pies that learn human languages with facility. To these he adds the birds of prey, eagles and falcons, among others, which Gaster domesticates and permits to return to the freedom of their element or fall back to earth as he chooses. His menagerie would not be complete without the animals of the earth and the fish of the sea. In listing them, Rabelais first includes the more noble animals such as the elephant and lion. To these he adds the bear, horse and dog. Then, having included the fish, he turns to whales and sea monsters. He completes the enumeration by naming the most savage of terrestrial beasts—wolves, bears, foxes, and serpents. "Et tout pour la trippe!"

The constantly recurring phrase of Rabelais's litany reminds us that Gaster tames and trains animals by controlling their food supply. Knowing that they will be rewarded, they learn to talk, hunt, dance, and jump about, leaving their proper element or natural habitats. Just as the enumeration progresses from the most docile birds to the most savage and monstrous beasts of earth and sea, there is a similar antithesis in the activities they learn. Beginning with the most characteristically human habit of speech, Rabelais concludes his listing by a reference to Hannibal, a reminder that animals have been trained for destructive warfare against men by men. The most monstrous beast trained by Gaster is man, who like Gaster can be insatiable ($QL/57$). "Et tout pour la trippe!"

Rabelais divides Gaster's followers, all who worship him as their god, into the two groups of Engastrimythes and Gastrolastres. The first are ventriloquists. Talking, not from their mouths, but from their stomachs, they are enchanters, divines who take advantage of the superstitious simple people for their own gain. The Gastrolastres are "tous ocieux, rien ne faisans, poinct ne travaillans, poys et charge inutile de la Terre." In two chapters Rabelais characterizes their materialism by a description of their meals, the menus for which consist of the most exotic courses (QL/58–60). "Et tout pour la trippe!"

Rabelais, like Pantagruel, holds these worshippers of Gaster "en grande abhomination." He compares them to Polyphemus to whom Euripides gives the words: "Je ne sacrifie que à *moy* (aux dieux poinct) et à cestuy mon ventre, le plus grand de tous les Dieux!" (QL/58). Thus Gaster takes on the semblance of self-love, which Rabelais detests, because *philautia* leads to blind bestiality.[27] Gaster, as "maistre es arts," also portrays bestiality, the lowest aspect of love. For he turns the sciences of medicine, astrology, and mathematics to self-gain. At his hands order becomes disorder, battle and counter-battle, mass destruction, pillage, and slaughter. Rabelais's enumeration of Gaster's accomplishments in the arts and sciences shows a progression similar to that of his menagerie.

Rabelais begins with Gaster's more useful accomplishments: cultivation of land to produce grain; medicine; astrology; the invention of military arts for the immediate protection of grain and related mathematical sciences used for long-range defense against natural calamities, beasts of prey, and brigands. To prepare wheat for eating Gaster invented windmills and similar engines, yeast, salt, fire, and the clock. When the supply of grain became insufficient, he found ways of transporting it and produced hybrid beasts of burden, chariots and carts, and boats. Unlimited in his capacity for knowledge, Gaster learned to control the elements to prevent storms that might destroy his crops. He built towns and fortresses to assure his own safety and that of his food supply. To these methods of protection he added all kinds of military machines, but he was no longer content just to maintain his own safety. He invented methods and equipment

for destroying cities and fortifications. Having begun his enumeration with those arts of Gaster that in this representative history of
man led to civilization, Rabelais thus concludes with those in-
ventions that destroy it. From grain, the staple of the human diet,
he progresses to the serpentine, monstrous cannon (QL/61–62).

Rabelais adds a final touch of irony to his listing of Gaster's
dubious accomplishments. As indicated by the title of the last
chapter of the episode, "Comment Gaster inventoit art et moyen
de non estre blessé ne touché par coups de Canon," Gaster's
supreme achievement is preservation of self against the forces
of disorder he himself set in motion. He invents a way to make
cannon balls stand in mid-air and turn against the enemy firing
them. But this discovery itself is undermined as Rabelais compares
it to a list of equally impossible acts from the world of fantasy of
ancient lore. The very "reality" of the world of Gaster's materialism disappears into the improbability of fantastic imagination.
Rabelais places in opposition to this realm of appearance that of
spiritual reality, which he suggests through an allegorical interpretation of the cock's song in the manner of the Pythagoreans
(QL/62). From physical disorder Rabelais returns to musical
and spiritual harmony; to bestiality he opposes *amor*. He does
not, however, imply any kind of asceticism as an alternate to
Gaster's materialism. Just as he shows through Pantagruel's example that riches are not evil within themselves, Rabelais gives
food and drink an important place in his work. They symbolize
the convivial society that is necessarily founded in *caritas*. Thus,
caritas itself takes on the meaning of *voluptas*.

The study of Rabelaisian *voluptas* entails, of necessity, an investigation of *gayeté d'esprit,* that aspect of *pantagruélisme* we
have not yet explored. No difficulty arises in associating a term
like *gayeté d'esprit* with Rabelais, who is best known for his
sense of humor. But the very range of his laughter, unless properly understood, leads to a shallow interpretation. It is not sufficient to stop at the surface, for Rabelais invites his reader to look
beyond the external pleasure of good humor to find not only its

cause but also the ultimate pleasure of which man is capable. We have seen that pleasure is the antithesis of absolute sensual hedonism. What remains for us to study is *gayeté* as humor, as playfulness, as play, and as contemplation.[28] For the term does point to such a hierarchy of acceptations for pleasure.

The humor implicit in Rabelais's *gayeté* manifests itself in too many ways to characterize here.[29] But whether as a subtle play on words or as the bitter ironic inversion of social satire, a sense of play pervades Rabelais's humor. The fantastic world of the gigantic that Rabelais conceived in his imagination is dominated by the playfulness of the creatures that inhabit it. The more serious aspects of their allegorical symbolism as well as the grossest eroticism of Rabelais's literary work have an underlying sense of play. That play itself has its basis in the dialectic of extremes as an examination of two examples of erotic humor will show.

The first example is seen in an anecdote that Panurge relates about a deaf-mute Roman lady. She mistakes the gestures of a man, who in reality asks her for directions, as an erotic invitation. She immediately takes him home and makes it plain to him that "le *jeu* luy plaisoit." The example is primarily of linguistic importance, for through it Rabelais shows that he refers to the preliminaries of love-making as play.[30] Similarly, Panurge's pursuit of the Parisian lady (*P*/21–22) gives a prime example of a double play. First the elaborate preparations of Panurge, his direct approach, and then his use of popularized Petrarchan/Platonic language, suggest the play aspect of love. His revenge through scenting the lady's dress with essence of bitch dogs in rut points to Rabelais's conception of the episode as ironic inversion and parody of the courtly Petrarchists and Platonists. Rabelais plays on the idea that the lady appears gentle and courteous, but in actuality she is no lady. Behind the literary play on appearance and reality we have seen the dialectic of opposites. Similarly, behind sexual play there is a dialogic opposition.

Huizinga has shown that sexual play exemplifies a cosmic agonic dualism.[31] It is a contest between the masculine and femi-

nine principles, which for Rabelais and his age underly the order
of macrocosm and microcosm. Rabelais symbolizes that contest
by the traditional dominance of the masculine Sun (reason) over
the feminine Moon (passion). He has Frère Jean, for example,
describe the Virgin clothed in the Sun and standing on the silver crescent (CL/34). And similarly in a specific kind of game—
the chess ballet—he has gold win out over silver contestants
(CL/24–25).[32] The symbolic contest through the opposition of
reason to passion points to the series of extremes of the dialectic
of opposites. The dialectic is not only a manifestation of play
but, in its highest sense, it is play itself as an examination of
voluptas will show.

The pleasure of Pantagruelian *gayeté d'esprit* is inextricably
bound to laughter, which Rabelais, following Aristotle, defines
as "le propre de l'homme." [33] Laughter, no matter what form it
takes, is a sign of play. In Rabelais it is usually associated with
conviviality, which affords the pleasure of an enjoyable exchange
of words *per se* or the intellectual companionship of wit and philosophical dialogue. Laughter stems from the *matieres joyeuses,*
which Rabelais ascribes to the literal level of *gayeté de cueur*
(G/Prol.). Laughter can be equally a sign of the *joye celeste* of
the Gargantuan Androgyna and of the *joyeuseté* of the contemplative experience of the Dive Bouteille (CL/34–44). In any
case, it can not be separated from Pantagruelian *caritas* and *sa-
pientia.*

That Rabelais conceived of Pantagruel as a philosophical sage
is apparent from the first chapter of Book III. There Rabelais
transforms the mischievous giant of folkloric tradition and of the
pranks of Book II into a philosopher-prince. By presenting the
end of the Dipsodian war in parallel with that of the Picrocholine
war, Rabelais not only suggests thematic parallelism of the first
two books but, more important, he points to an essential similar-
ity between Gargantua and Pantagruel. He emphasizes the charitable aspects of Pantagruel's treatment of the conquered Dip-
sodians. He adds to that picture of the charitable prince a new

dimension, for Rabelais also describes Pantagruel as an angel, a hero, and a daimon, much as Alcibiades portrays Socrates.

The dimension Rabelais adds to *caritas* is implicit in the Platonic conception of the philosopher. Socrates as the embodiment of the intermediary Love fulfills the highest goal of man—contemplation. Contemplation is the completion of the triad Beauty-Love-*Voluptas* described by Ficino in the *Commentarium*:

> Circulus itaque unus et idem a deo in mundum, a mundo in deum, tribus nominibus nuncupatur. Prout in deo incipit et allicit, pulchritude; prout in mundum transiens ipsum rapit, amor; coniungit, voluptas.[34]

In the philosophical context inspired by the *Republic,* the relationship of the higher spiritual *voluptas* to contemplation is expressed in a dialogue attributed to Rabelais by Le Caron.

Among his Platonically oriented prose *Dialogues* (1556), Louis Le Caron includes the "Valton, de la tranquillité d'esprit ou du souverain bien" where he relates a dialogue between Rabelais, Valton (Le Caron's uncle) and Cotereau. Rabelais first disavows any adherence to the school of Epicurus or any other sect. Stating the principle that "chacune chose aspire à son dernier et souverain contentement, le quel aiant obtenu lors elle ne desire daventege," he proceeds to show that true *volupté* (the spiritual *voluptas*) consists of harmony among the three kinds of *volupté* that correspond to the three souls of man. The *souveraine volupté* is that which leads to truth. Corresponding to Ficino's celestial Love, it is the *volupté* that governs the other two and instills harmony and temperance in man. The origin and end of this higher pleasure is "la cognoissance des choses divines et plus excellentes, et son propre devoir de rendre l'homme content selon la parfaite nature."[35]

Whether or not one accepts this dialogue as an authentic account of Rabelais's words as does Pinvert[36] or as a judgment on Rabelais's philosophical interest as Marcel de Grève seems to conclude,[37] it is apparent that there is no essential disaccord between Rabelais's thought expressed in his novel and the dialogue. The

"Valton," which shows a correct interpretation of Epicurus and Pico, serves as a good summary of Rabelais's thought implicit in the voyage theme and in the symbolism of the Dive Bouteille.[38] For the ultimate pleasure man can attain is contemplation and knowledge "des choses divines."

Contemplation is not, however, for Rabelais an end in itself. Just as human love leads to procreation and corporeal immortality, love of truth and knowledge carries with it the desire to teach and write to ensure a certain intellectual immortality for the philosopher.[39] Ficino thus combines the active and the contemplative lives. Rabelais, in turn, emphasizes the active role of the philosopher, as exemplified in Bacbuc's benediction to the departing visitors:

> Allez, amis, en protection de ceste sphere intellectuelle de laquelle en tous lieux est le centre et n'a en lieu aucun circonferance, que nous appellons Dieu: et venus en vostre monde portez tesmoignage que sous terre sont les grands tresors et choses admirables (CL/47).

Thus, the metaphysical cycle of love flowing from and returning to God has its parallel on the level of human experience.

Both contemplation and interpretation are part of the Rabelaisian dialectic. Love of divine wisdom is the ultimate fulfillment of man. Although in a certain sense, as Socrates suggests in the *Republic,* the pursuit of wisdom involves philosophical dialectic, that aspect of dialectic eludes definition.[40] Contemplation is an intuitive experience that in the Platonic sense involves those faculties of man beyond human nature. *Voluptas,* in fact, dialectically links God and man. Contemplation is the ultimate dialectic that expresses itself in a play between man and God. As Meister Eckhart points out in one of his sermons, "God plays and laughs in good deeds."[41] Through the humanity of Christ that tension that exists between Creator and creature is alleviated, and man returns to his source. Through love he completes himself in God and through love he turns back to the world. Love of knowledge leads to God in contemplation and actively returns to the world as *agapé*. The relationship "God:creature:God" is thought of as active, "man:God:man," and expresses itself in the relationships "man:man" and "microcosm:macrocosm." The philosopher must interpret his contemplative vision, teaching man about himself and his relationship to other men, to the world and to God. He accomplishes this task of interpretation through myth and symbol.

For Rabelais and for Plato philosophical interpretation of the intuitive contemplative experience is impossible. Man can not express in rational terms what is beyond discursive reason. The philospher can not describe his vision of absolute truth; therefore he must become a poet. Through his imagination he must create another nonreal world that symbolizes, even so, the real world. Through image, myth, and allegory he approximates the dialectical vision of intuition. Through the discourse of poetic form he plays.[42] He plays with God and man in a contemplative and active fulfillment of *caritas*. Through the play of dialectic he accomplishes the link between the extremes. Rabelais finds in *caritas* and *pantagruélisme,* which he expresses poetically in the allegorical myths associated with the Androgyna and the *pantagruelion,* the fullest expression of that dialectical ideal.

In summary, then, the play on appearance and reality of all Rabelais's images and symbols is grounded in the Platonic dialectic of the coincidence of opposites. Allegorical myths in Rabelais express that dialectic and the play that lies behind it. Symbols and myths bridge the gap between the realms of absolute truth (Ideas) and the world of appearances (forms). The philosopher who achieves the highest end of man in contemplating divine reality plays on the tension between intellect and matter in expressing poetically his intuitive vision. In Rabelais's work the myths of Gargantua and Pantagruel convey their creator's ideal of *caritas*. Love, in turn, not only serves as a link between God and man and the totality of creation, but is also the ultimate fulfillment of man. The dialectic of opposites is not only Rabelais's literary means of expression, but also his ideal.

The study of images and myths in this first chapter has led to an exploration of the use and ideal conception of Rabelaisian dialectic in reference to Platonism. The investigation of *play* touched upon the convivial aspects of dialogue, but the full implications of dialogue *per se* remain unexamined. They will be the subject of the following chapter and will be discussed in the light of the transformation of *homo ridens* to *homo bibens*.

NOTES

1. Plato, *The Symposium*, 212c–223d. See Erasmus, *Chiliadis tertiae, Centuria III, Opera omnia*, II, 770D–771B; and Lefranc, "Notes pour le commentaire," *RER*, VII (1909), 433–39.

2. The precious drugs of Rabelais's version correspond to the figurines of gods in Plato and to the *numen* in Erasmus' text.

3. Etienne Gilson, "Rabelais franciscain," in *Les Idées et les lettres*, pp. 201–202. See Ezechiel 17, and also Augustin Renaudet, *Préréforme et humanisme à Paris pendant les premières guerres d'Italie (1494–1517)*, p. 55.

4. For a discussion of Augustine's *De doctrina christiana*, on which the doctrine of sense and sentence is primarily based, and related literature, see Bernard F. Huppé, *Doctrine and Poetry: Augustine's Influence on Old English Poetry*, pp. 3–27, *et pass.* Erich Auerbach's comments on "Figura," *Scenes from the Drama of European Literature*, pp. 11–76, remain the best source of information on the figural.

5. See Giovanni Pico della Mirandola, *Heptaplus, Opera*, foll. I^r–II^r, and Angelo Poliziano, "Oratio in expositione Homere," *Omnia opera*, foll. LVI^r–LXII^r.

6. Leo Hebraeus, "Dialogo Secondo," *Dialoghi d'amore*, ed. Carl Gebhardt, foll. 26^v–30^r, and *De l'amour*, trans. Pontus de Tyard, I, 175–83. Florence May Weinberg, "Rabelais and Christian Hermetism, the Wine and the Will" (unpublished doctoral dissertation), discusses the hermetic aspects of Rabelaisian symbolism and allegory in detail, especially pp. 8–42.

7. Jean Seznec, *The Survival of the Pagan Gods: The Mythological Tradition and its Place in Renaissance Humanism and Art*, trans. Barbara F. Sessions, pp. 84–121.

8. Jehan Thenaud, *La Lignée de Saturne*, and *Traité de poesie*. See also E. H. Gombrich, "Botticelli's Mythologies: A Study in the Neoplatonic Symbolism of his Circle," *Journal of the Warburg and Courtauld Institutes*, VIII (1945), 22–37; and Seznec, *Survival of the Pagan Gods*, pp. 219–56.

9. Marcel Tetel, *Rabelais*, pp. 88–89, somewhat ambiguously tends to negate the allegorical interpretation of Rabelais.

10. Tetel, *Rabelais*, p. 86.

11. A more extensive discussion of these images will be found in my article, "The Hermetic and Platonic Traditions," pp. 15–29.

12. E. H. Gombrich, "Icones Symbolicae, The Visual Image in Neo-Platonic Thought," *The Journal of the Warburg and Courtauld Institutes*, XI (1948), 163–92.

13. For a discussion of Renaissance hieroglyphs and related bibliography, see my article, "Rabelais and Renaissance Figure Poems," *Etudes rabelaisiennes*, VIII, 39–54.

14. Plato, *Cratylus*, 389d–393d, 430d–439d, *Timaeus*, 30c–32c, 47d/e. See also Jean Guiton, "Le Mythe des paroles gelées," *Romanic Review*, XXXI (1940), 3–15; and Leo Spitzer, "Rabelais et les 'rabelaisants,' " *Studi Francesi*, IV (1960), 402–405.

15. I Cor. 13:4–5 and *cf.* Plattard, in Rabelais, *Gargantua*, viii, t. I, 90, and n. 95.

16. Plato, *Symposium*, 189d–193d; Leo Hebraeus, *Dialoghi*, III, ed. Gebhardt, foll. 81ro–93vo, *De l'amour*, trans. Tyard, II, 222–53. See also Maurice Scève, "Microcosme," *Œuvres poétiques complètes*, ed. Bertrand Guégan, p. 197; Antoine Héroët, "L'Androgyne de Platon," *Œuvres poétiques*, ed. Ferdinand Gohin, STFM, pp. 71–89; Ficino, *Commentaire sur le Banquet de Platon*, ed. and trans. Raymond Marcel, pp. 201–203; and Edgar Wind, *Pagan Mysteries in the Renaissance*, pp. 165–66. Weinberg, "Rabelais and Christian Hermetism," discusses the comical and serious aspects of the Androgyna as a symbol. On the concept of love-harmony, see Leo Spitzer, *Classical and Christian Ideas of World Harmony*, ed. Anna Granville Hatcher, pp. 5–63; Kristeller, *Philosophy of Marsilio Ficino*, pp. 74–99, 263–87; Gombrich, "Icones Symbolicae," 163–92; Erwin Panofsky, *Studies in Iconology: Humanistic Themes in the Art of the Renaissance*, pp. 99–101, 141–53; and Pico, *Heptaplus*, foll. I^r–XX^r.

17. Plato, *Timaeus*, 27d–43b, 69c–71c; *Phaedrus*, 246a–249b.

18. *Cf.* K. H. Francis, "Rabelais and Mathematics," *BHR*, XXI (1959), 88, and Spitzer, *Classical and Christian Ideas*, pp. 11–12.

19. *Republic*, 614a–617d, *Timaeus*, 27d–39e.

20. *Republic*, 521c–535a.

21. *Cf.* Festugière, *Philosophie de l'amour*, pp. 41–53, and Edward F. Meylan, "L'évolution de la notion d'amour platonique," *HR*, V (1938), 419–32.

22. Marichal, "L'Attitude de Rabelais devant le Néoplatonisme,"

185–87, and M. A. Screech, "An Interpretation of the *Querelle des Amyes,*" *BHR,* XXI (1959), 125–26.

23. Cassirer, *Individual and the Cosmos,* pp. 24–32, 62–71. For a discussion of Renaissance attitudes toward wealth, see Hans Baron, "Franciscan Poverty and Civic Wealth as Factors in the Rise of Humanistic Thought," *Speculum,* XIII (1938), 1–37.

24. *Cf.* Dante Alighieri, *Inferno,* Canto VII, *The Divine Comedy,* ed. and trans. John D. Sinclair, I, 98–105, and Sinclair, "Notes," pp. 106–108.

25. *Cf.* Dante, *Inferno,* Cantos XIV, XVII, I, 180–87, 214–21, and Sinclair, "Notes," 189–91, 222–24.

26. *Cf.* Ficino, *Commentaire sur le Banquet,* III, iii, p. 163, V, xiii, p. 198; Marichal, "Rabelais devant le Néoplatonisme," 186; and Screech, "The *Querelle des Amyes,*" 127–29.

27. *Cf.* Rabelais's correspondence with Tiraqueau, *Œuvres complètes,* ed. Boulenger, pp. 976, 979.

28. Much of the discussion on play reflects the comments of Johan Huizinga, *Homo ludens: A Study of the Play-Element in Culture.* It would be well to recall Huizinga's definition of *play* here: "Play is a voluntary activity or occupation executed within certain fixed limits of time and place, according to rules freely accepted but absolutely binding, having its aim in itself and accompanied by a feeling of tension, joy and the consciousness that it is 'different' from 'ordinary life.'" (p. 28). See also his comment, "Nothing could be more playful than Rabelais—he is the play-spirit incarnate." (p. 181).

29. For a good introductory study to Rabelaisian humor, see Marcel Tetel, *Etude sur le comique de Rabelais.*

30. Huizinga, *Homo ludens,* p. 43.

31. Huizinga, *Homo ludens,* pp. 53–63.

32. For a discussion of the alchemical symbolism of gold and silver, see *infra,* pp. 57, 83, 90, 93.

33. Aristotle, *Parts of Animals,* III, x, 673a; Rabelais, *Gargantua,* "Aux lecteurs," ll. 10–11; t. I, p. 2, and n. 7. See also Huizinga, *Homo ludens,* p. 6.

34. Ficino, *Commentaire sur le Banquet,* II, ii, p. 146.

35. Lucien Pinvert, "Un entretien philosophique de Rabelais rapporté par Charondas (1556)," *RER,* I (1903), 193–99.

36. Pinvert, "Entretien philosophique," 193, and "Louis Le Caron, dit Charondas (1536–1613)," *Revue de la Renaissance,* II (1902), 5.

37. Marcel de Grève, *L'Interprétation de Rabelais au XVIᵉ siècle,* pp. 133–35.

38. See D. C. Allen, "The Rehabilitation of Epicurus and His Theory of Pleasure in the Early Renaissance," *Studies in Philology,* XLI (1944), 1–15.

39. Ficino, *Commentaire sur le Banquet,* VI, xi, pp. 223–25.

40. *Republic,* 531d–535a.

41. *Meister Eckhart,* trans. Raymond Bernard Blakney, 143–45, and "Legends," p. 251, for a similar reference.

42. See Ludwig Edelstein, "The Function of the Myth in Plato's Philosophy," *Journal of the History of Ideas,* X (1949), 464–73, and Huizinga, *Homo ludens,* pp. 105–172.

abelais, like Plato, associates the philosophical dialogue with wine. Although he models his own *convivium* on Plato's *symposion* (*TL/* 36), he does not strictly follow the two-part division of the Greek banquet. For Plato the *potos* or *sympotos,* the drinking session that succeeds the dinner itself (*deipnon* or *syndeipnon*), was the more important part.[1] But, whereas Rabelais begins his dialogue during dinner (*TL/*29-30), he follows Plato's example in having his *convives* drink together literally and figuratively. For Rabelais and for Plato the *symposion* serves as the framework for the intellectual exchange of ideas in the pursuit of truth. For both the wine symbolism of the *convivium* has, beyond the level of philosophical dialogue, a literal level of *conviviality* and a metaphysical level of *imbibing truth*. (Drinking for its opiate effect, obviously very important in Rabelais, is not dealt with here.)

A casual reminder suffices to recall to Rabelais's reader the literal level of wine. Rabelais begins his work by a playful invitation to his "Beuveurs tres illustres" (*G*/Prol.). Some form of *boire* recurs as a constant motif throughout the five books by reference to wine and drinking or in scenes of carousing and more elevated social conviviality. But the pleasure of drinking in good company does not imply approval of drunkenness. Rabelais rejects the image of a drunken Socrates. Similarly, although Rabelais takes no exception to being compared to Horace in expressing in his work more the spirit of imaginative wine than scholarly oil, he obviously gives a symbolic meaning to his statement (*G*/Prol.). And when he suggests figuratively that writing his book took no more time than his corporal nourishment, "sçavoir est beuvant et mengeant," he points once more to the metaphorical meaning of drinking.

In the "Prologue" to *Gargantua,* as in the introductory epigraph to his humanistic edition of Hippocrates and Galen, Rabelais appeals to his reader to drink from the deep fount of knowledge.[2] Such an appeal reflects the spirit of *pantagruelisant,* which

is initially defined as "beuvans à gré et lisant les gestes horrific-
ques de Pantagruel" (*G/*1). But Rabelais transforms the Pantagruel of legend from the mischievous devil of medieval farces
who went about instilling thirst by sprinkling salt in sleepers'
throats into a philosopher-prince.[3] Similarly the *beuvans* of *pantagruélisme* assumes the philosophical meaning of Plato's *Symposium: in vino veritas.*[4] Rabelais reflects that metaphysical
meaning of wine in his own adaptation of the motto *"en vin
verité"* for the Temple de la Dive Bouteille (*CL/*37). It is equally
present in his *fontaine Caballine* of the "Prologue" to Book III:

> Attendez un peu que je hume quelque traict de ceste
> bouteille: c'est mon vray et seul Helicon, c'est ma fontaine
> Caballine, c'est mon unicque enthusiasme. Icy beuvant je
> *delibere,* je *discours,* je *resoulz* et *concluds.* (My italics)

The emphasis is on *drinking,* for whether wine, nectar, or water
is drunk there is no difference in the symbolism.[5] In equating
the three images at the metaphysical level, Rabelais uses for his
own ends the traditional imagery of the mysteries.

In the Bacchic mysteries of death and resurrection wine symbolizes the fountain of life.[6] Plato, adapting the mysteries to
philosophical purpose, makes of wine a fountain of intuitive
knowledge and expresses his connotation through the Dionysian
furor.[7] Similar usages of wine naturally pervade Christian ritual
and mysticism. For example, the wine of the Eucharist, because
it embodies the blood of Christ, is the fountain of life and grace.[8]
In the long line of Christian mystical symbolism Santa Teresa
equates the water God pours on the garden of her soul with the
contemplative inebriation of wine.[9] Rabelais, in giving wine its
fullest meaning, draws on all these traditions and transforms
them through his own myth of the voyage to the Dive Bouteille
into a philosophical experience of dialectic.

Dialogue and wine are thus inextricably bound together in
Rabelais's literary symbolism, as may be shown by reference to
the three most salient characteristics of man-at-drink. *Homo ridens* portrays on the literal level of wine imagery the convivial

aspect of human dialogue. *Homo colloquens* embodies the philosophical dialectic of Rabelais's symposium. And *homo bibens*
gives the fullest expression of the intuitive dialogue through the
symbolic poetic furor of Dionysian mysteries.

1. *HOMO RIDENS:* CONVIVIALITY, THE PLEASURE OF DRINKING

Dialogue at the literal level of conviviality could hardly imply
more than conversation. It might involve wit and certainly always
includes good humor, for both are aspects of Rabelaisian play.
Conviviality, an attitude founded in a spirit of play, reflects the
principles of Rabelaisian *caritas* and of *pantagruélisme*. Since
Rabelais begins his work by a reminder of Aristotle's definition of
man and by an appeal to drink, *homo ridens* appropriately characterizes the conviviality of Pantagruel and Gargantua.

Gargantua's first words, "A boyre! à boyre! à boyre!" are particularly suitable to the occasion of his birth (*G*/6). He comes
into the world after a lively tippling session, an excellent example of Rabelais's ability to portray "au vif" the conversation of his
day. Having completed dinner Grandgousier and his companions adjourn to the willow grove where they "entrerent en propos de resieuner on propre lieu." Rabelais describes the lively
scene of trotting bottles, flying goblets, and emptying jugs, cap-
turing the spirit of convivial merriment.

The conversation begins as drinkers ask the page for wine:
"Tire!—Baille!—Tourne!—Brouille!—Boutte à moy sans eau;
ainsi mon amy! . . . Produiz moy du clairet, verre pleurant."
With the interjection "Treves de soif!"—another request for
wine—the dialogue turns to drinking itself and the cause of
drinking, thirst, as suggested by the reply, "Ha, faulse fiebvre,
ne t'en iras tu pas?" But first there is an aside. Perhaps addressed
to Gargamelle, the query "Vous estez morfondue, m'amie?" and
its answer, "Voire," may be a reference to Gargamelle's condi-

tion and a forewarning of her sudden illness. The conversation resumes immediately, "Ventre sainct Quenet! parlons de boire!" As though in protest to the moment of gravity, the speaker insists on a subject suitable to the festive occasion.

The Franciscan begins, "Je ne boy que à mes heures, comme la mulle du pape." He plays on the triple significance of *heures* as religious devotions, as appropriateness of time, and as a book of hours, which like the "breviaire" of the retort may be understood as a bottle. Resuming the question of thirst proposed earlier, someone (perhaps a cleric) asks which was first, thirst or drink. With the first answer the conversation turns to Scholastic theology, "Soif; car qui eust beu sans soif durant le temps de innocence?" A cleric, however, opposes this position, quoting from law, "Beuverye, car *privatio presupponit habitum [et nihil potest esse prius in privatione quam sit in habitu]*." Then someone comments on the previous speaker's question, "Nous aultres innocens ne beuvons que trop sans soif." This comment is, of course, the inversion of innocence, just as the next retort through fallacious logic transposes future thirst to the present, and thereby "saves" a witty sinner.

In addition to presenting a witty play on Scholastic logic, Rabelais proposes here a more serious study by raising the question of appetite and drunkenness. Man before the Fall would have indulged only moderately his thirst or sensual appetite for wine. Similarly, the reasonable, temperate man only satisfies his thirst; he never drinks excessively. The comment, "Beuverye, car *privatio supponit habitum*," must necessarily refer to man after the Fall. It would be justifiable to say possession (*habitum*) precedes absence of the thing possessed; but, within terms of Scholastic philosophy, desire (*i.e.,* thirst) or knowledge of the thing desired comes first. The answer is therefore more philosophically correct. The attribution of innocence to himself by the speaker who drinks too much without thirst exemplifies humor through inversion. The next speaker recognizes this sin of excessiveness, but he claims innocence for his own sin of philosophical hypocrisy.

By the clever device of continually imagining future thirst, he satisfies each moment of future thirst in the present, thereby remaining technically sober but capable of intoxication.

The remainder of the dialogue presents similar wit, fallacious logic, and plays on words. The modes of thought range from theology to pornography. The speakers represent various levels of society: the king and queen, their page and governess, soldiers, lawyers, clerics, friars and priests.[10] The scene is a good example of the acceptable form of conviviality basic to the symbols *vin* and *pantagruelisant*. For these symbols imply a dialectical duality of which the extremes are wine, or drinking *per se,* and the metaphorical imbibing of intuitive truth. Wine as the material symbol implies an acceptance of companionable drinking. Just as Renaissance dualism leads to a positive re-evaluation and acceptance of the world and body as things good within themselves, so society and the mutual relations among men take on new meaning. Wine itself is not evil. But excessive drinking, as exemplified by the Gastrolastres, is a form of sensual materialism and Rabelais soundly condemns it. Moderation, as Gargantua learns from Ponocrates, must be applied in drinking as in every action.[11] So wine when used properly leads to pleasurable conversation and good humor in a *selective* society. That society is by definition limited to *pantagruelistes;* it is represented, of course, by Theleme.

In dualistic terms, Theleme takes on new meaning. It expresses Rabelais's ideal of social relations within a selected society. Young men and women of grace, beauty, and charm, dressed elegantly and harmoniously, live in pleasing surroundings. They play, study, and *drink* together in mutual amiability. The "antimonasticism" of Theleme emphasizes the importance of an active social life within the present. Rabelais, while criticizing the hypocrisy of monks who do not live up to their vows, shows that members of a society guided by *caritas,* which insists on mutual understanding and intrinsic individual honor, can achieve more than those who merely wear the habit of the monk.

In describing the activities of the Thelemites, Rabelais gives particular importance to drinking. Since Theleme is an educational center, drinking in addition to suggesting conviviality implies a way of learning. For Rabelais, as for Plato in the *Laws,* drinking signifies temperate ebriety.[12] Just as the exemplary guardian learns to overcome his fear through constant exposure to danger, Rabelais's philosophical *pantagrueliste* gains knowledge of pleasure through exposure to it. In the company of his *gentilz compaignons* he learns to avoid excess and drunkenness, to drink in moderation (*G*/54–57). Wine is also rejuvenatory. It frees the imagination from those restraints of probity which accompany age, making the drinker more joyful and more hopeful, and giving him renewed faith in the freedom and liberty of his intellect. Wine thereby leads to dialogic truth in both its meaning for the contemplative individual and in its convivial application. And the attitude of companionly conversation seen in the playful exchange of conviviality is a necessary part of dialogue at the literal level of simple conversation and at the more elevated level of philosophical dialogue.

2. *HOMO COLLOQUENS:* THE INTELLECTUAL DISCOURSE OF THE SYMPOSIUM

The formal philosophical *convivium* of Rabelais's *Tiers Livre* occupies only a few chapters (*TL*/29–36), but it contains, nevertheless, the central and dominant theme of the book. In a sense, the early chapters devoted to divinatory consultations (*TL*/9–28) foreshadow the philosophical dialogue, and the later chapters suggest the fullest meaning of dialectic through folly and an anticipation of the voyage theme (*TL*/37–52). But dialogue is not only the theme of Book III; it also affords the primary means by which Rabelais sets forth the importance of dialectic. He suggests three types of dialogue reflected in divination, philosophical discourse, and folly, and associated, respectively, with the unconscious, conscious, and intuitive metaconscious modes of *homo colloquens.*

Of these three types of dialogue the most ancient and the most primitive is divination (*TL*/9–28). An external, indirect means to truth, it requires a mediating agent to convey and/or interpret divine will. Divination is a one-way form of communication in which there is a vertical relationship between the interlocutor and God. By its very nature it is usually uncertain and ambiguous. Like all forms of dialogue, divination requires a sincere willingness on the part of the seeker to learn. But Panurge lacks both the will and the ability to accept truth. In all the consultations his reaction and that of Pantagruel establish a pattern.[13] Pantagruel interprets the oracular signs negatively. He sees Panurge cuckolded if he should marry. As one would expect, Panurge irascibly refuses to listen. He paints a glowing picture of a happy marriage filled with erotic contentment. Panurge's anger, similar to that of Picrochole, points to his inversion of the dialogic basis. Dominated by his sensual appetite, Panurge's microcosmic intellect is necessarily erratic and has alienated him from himself, from his fellow man, and from God. In "seeking truth" Panurge inverts the principle of dialogue, for no matter how willing he is to find truth, until he becomes attuned to himself he cannot expect to enter charitably into a meaningful relationship with others. Until he *wills* to know himself and his place in the divine scheme of things instead of trying to exert his own will he can not find truth. Therefore, Panurge dooms any attempt at discourse whether through divination or philosophical dialogue to failure.

Panurge's role as interrogator in the symposium of Book III presents a prime example of ironic inversion of the Socratic dialogue. Panurge, unlike Socrates who personifies truth, can not even look for it in proper perspective because his slavery to passion unfavorably prejudices his quest. He therefore inverts the principle of the Socratic *conosce te ipsum* that Rabelais has established as the main theme of the banquet. Rabelais has Pantagruel invite a theologian, a philosopher, a physician, and a jurisconsult, corresponding to the four levels of intellection of Plato's

Republic.[14] Each of the interlocutors counsels Panurge to seek out his own will. Pantagruel sets the theme (*TL*/29) and Hippothadée echos the same advice at the inception of the dialogue (*TL*/30). Rondibilis tells Panurge to learn of his physical limitations (*TL*/31), and Trouillogan insists on self-knowledge and self-control (*TL*/36). They agree with Hippothadée that a wife mirrors her husband, and Panurge's wife would accordingly reflect his intemperate passion and irrational conduct. Recognizing his friend's *philautia,* Pantagruel had conceived the symposium so that his companion might learn to know himself spiritually, mentally, and physically through dialogic consultations.

Panurge refuses, however, to turn the dialogues to examination of self. He almost proudly points out his own concupiscence and rejects as an impossibility Hippothadée's clear advice about his being cuckolded (*TL*/30). Panurge listens to Rondibilis' factual medical enumeration of the five ways to overcome carnal lust. But he will have no part of wine, drugs, assiduous labor, and fervent study. He has accepted in advance the fifth means, the sexual act itself. He refuses to recognize his own age and that he should act with moderation. Instead of applying the physician's advice to himself as a means of overcoming lust, he rather finds in marriage a way of indulging it. His sensual desire has not been lessened, but increased by the consultation (*TL*/31). He similarly refuses to accept Trouillogan's suggestion that he consult himself.

Trouillogan's dialogue with Panurge poses several problems of interpretation. First of all his advice is ambiguous. His conversation with Panurge makes a complete circle without any resolution other than a paradoxical yes-and-no answer. Up to the time of Gragantua's sudden entry into the dialogue, Trouillogan elicits a positive reaction from the other *convives,* except, of course, Panurge. As Rondibilis suggests, the philosopher mirrors the Cusanan doctrine of extremes:

> Ainsi (dist Rondibilis) mettons nous neutre en medicine et moyen en philosophie, par participation de l'une et l'aultre extremité, par abnegation de l'une et l'aultre extremité et,

par compartiment du temps, maintenant en l'une, maintenant en l'aultre extremité.

But as Trouillogan continues the dialogue with facetious responses, the giants and their company show disapproval of the
philosopher.

Except for his sound advice to Panurge that he do what he
wills and his related refusal to give him other counsel, Trouillogan's answers are all evasive. Like the oracles, he offers no philosophical clarification for his position. He dismisses simple questions that he could answer affirmatively or negatively and then
clarify with illustrations. For example, when Panurge asks if he
had been married before, he replies, "Possible est." And he answers, "Il n'est pas impossible," when asked if he found his first
marriage agreeable. But Panurge is not the only one present who
finds the philosopher evasive. Gargantua ends the dialogue with
a tirade against Pyrrhonism and shows his disapproval by leaving
the banquet hall (*TL*/36).

This scene presents a good example of the serious and humorous aspects of Rabelaisian play. Through an inversion of the Socratic dialogue, Rabelais has Panurge ask the questions. But, in
the final analysis, the philosopher plays with Panurge. Fully
aware of Panurge's dilemma, Trouillogan refuses to give him a
solution. Panurge reacts with his customary anger; he swears in
vain. The consultation is a game of cat and mouse in which the
philosopher toys with his consultant. It ends in irresolution, partly
because Trouillogan knows that Panurge must find his own solution, partly because the philosopher himself can not reach a decision about his own affairs. Thus, in the end, Rabelais plays with
both Panurge and Trouillogan, for in his comic vision of their
game the blind leads the blind.

The Pyrrhonism represented by Trouillogan contradicts antithetically Pantagruel's continued advice to Panurge that he make
an intellectually sound decision and remain firm in it. Trouillogan in constantly weighing all the possibilities never comes to any
solution except another possibility. Through his criticism of the

philosopher Rabelais censures the growing tendency in the sixteenth century toward skepticism and Pyrrhonism. He opposes
philosophy that leads through irresolution to inaction. But his
criticism of Pyrrhonism does not imply a rejection of Cusanus'
theory of the coincidence of opposites. Rabelais and Cusanus, like
Trouillogan, conceive of truth as elusive, but Rabelais insists upon
an active involvement in attaining it. And he finds in the philosophy of extremes the doctrine of learned ignorance and wise folly.

After the banquet has broken up, Pantagruel proposes a third
type of dialogue to Panurge. Realizing that all the previous divinatory and philosophical consultations have failed to bring his
companion to self-knowledge, Pantagruel suggests one final possibility—to seek counsel of a madman or fool. He reminds Panurge that many rulers have benefited from the wisdom of their
fools. He contrasts with the "saige mondain" the fool, who is not
wise in the eyes of men but "en l'estimation des intelligences
coelestes" (TL/37). Rabelais thus reminds his readers that human knowledge within itself only reflects truth. Man can not attain absolute wisdom, which pertains to God alone. In thinking
that he has gained certainty man becomes ridiculous. Though he
may seem wise to his fellow men he remains foolish before divine
wisdom.

For Rabelais, as for Cusanus, dialectic extremes are resolved in
the infinite wisdom of God. But man can not approach understanding of the Infinite through human discursive reason. Only
through intellectual vision can he attain knowledge of the divine. That vision is limited, moreover, to momentary, and partial
intuitions. Man does not contemplate the divine with angelic intellect in completion and in continuity. He is, however, endowed
with intellect akin to that of the angels; but to attain a contemplative vision of the Infinite, he must free himself from his body
through divinely inspired furor.[15] Rabelais's adaptation of the Platonic poetic furor as a forgetting-of-self and a going-out-of-oneself
does not contradict the idea of self-knowledge and interiority of
experience. For as the symbolism of the Dive Bouteille shows,

Rabelais views the seeming external furor as an inner intellectual vision. Man's greatest folly is his failure to realize that he becomes himself only through fulfilling the potentiality of that vision. Without it and by comparison with it the best of human knowledge is ignorance.

The *Tiers Livre,* especially Rabelais's praise of folly, owes much to the *Encomium Moriae.*[16] The influence of Erasmus is particularly noticeable in the litany of folly where Rabelais attributes the ridiculous aspects of the human comedy, as well as the positive characteristics of furor, to Triboullet. Pantagruel and Panurge vie with one another to have the last word. Through a series of epithets, either complementary or antithetical, they themselves attain a kind of folly. Although Rabelais achieves a comic effect by the exuberance of enumeration, he also points to the philosophical basis of furor.[17] The blazoning starts with Pantagruel's suggestion that Triboullet is "competentement fol." Pantagruel then begins a series inspired by the astrological influences which determine madness, "F[ol] fatal, . . . de nature, . . . celeste, . . . jovial, . . . mercurial, . . . lunaticque, . . . erraticque, . . . eccentricque, . . . aeteré et junonien, . . . articque." The list consistently and logically follows the first attribute, for by means of celestial influences Providence determines the fate of men. Pantagruel associates folly with three of the planets. Triboullet owes his madness to his natal house of Jupiter. His variability comes from Mercury, his instability and irrationality from the Moon. Unable to bring constancy and order into his life, he wanders like the planets. His soul does not show the regularity of circular movement, but rather the eccentricity of a planet out of its orbit. His element is air. The zodiacal signs of the Northern Hemisphere dominate him.

Panurge begins his responses with musical terminology, closely associated with the astrological lyre of Orpheus: "F[ol] de haulte game, . . . de *b* quarre et de *b* mol." His attribution of terrestriality to Triboullet both contradicts and complements Pantagruel's epithet, "celeste." There are two kinds of folly, one a divinely inspired or celestial furor, the other the purely human folly of self-love and pretentious learnedness. To these, of course, must be added madness, which has the same external manifestations as furor. Triboullet, because of his madness, is a "f[ol] terrien;" as a representative of furor, he is a "f[ol] celeste." Panurge next selects attributes that result from Pantagruel's characterizations. Triboullet is "joyeulx et folastrant" because of the Jovian influence, "jolly et folliant" because he is "mercurial." Panurge then introduces a series of ornamental descriptions which, in addition to suggesting details of a jester's costume, are rhymed in the manner of the Rhetoriqueurs: "f[ol] à pompettes, . . . à pilettes, . . . à sonnettes." He counters Pantagruel's epithet "aeteré et junonien" with "riant et venerien," opposing the passionate lustfulness and earthly pleasure represented by Venus to the marital fidelity of the more austere Juno. Panurge's response to "f[ol] arcticque," in addition to beginning a series of adjectives based on winemaking, stems antithetically from the superior Northern Hemisphere.

With "f[ol] heroicque, . . . genial, . . . praedestiné," the specially chosen superior men, Pantagruel begins a long series depicting, in descending hierarchical order, the secular, political, and social ranks, both noble and common, of the human comedy. Panurge counters with an ecclesiastical series that corresponds in order and includes representative members of the hierarchy of scholars, priests, monks and clerics (*TL*/38). Rabelais, thus following the example of Erasmus, presents man as a masked actor strutting about on the stage of life. Like Erasmus he also presents the folly of human knowledge from metaphysics to pheonasm, the inanity of logic and the emptiness of form.[18] Rabelais's depiction of human knowledge as folly does not imply a separation of reason and faith or a tendency toward fideism, as critics have recently suggested.[19] For him, as for Cusanus, human science complements intuitive knowledge; but the human disciplines are insufficient within themselves. When Rabelais turns to folly he follows the example of Erasmus and Cornelius Agrippa. Agrippa's

De incertitudine et vanitate scientiarum is not a work of skepticism. Rather it attacks those who rely solely on human knowledge and seek through it to raise themselves above the human condition. The treatise is not fideistic. Agrippa, like Rabelais, accepts the human disciplines with proper humility and with the realization that all knowledge depends on God.[20] This is the significance Rabelais gives to folly in the episodes of Bridoye and Triboullet.

Folly strengthens the parallel between Rabelais's *convivium* and Plato's *Symposium*. For, just as Plato uses Diotima to show that divine revelation is the source of Socrates' knowledge of Love, so Rabelais presents the judge Bridoye to demonstrate that knowledge and justice are of divine origin.[21] Bridoye does not figure within the *convivium* proper, but he is one of the invited guests. He is unable to attend because he himself has been summoned to stand trial before the high court to be questioned about an unjust sentence he gave. Pantagruel shows particular interest in Bridoye, not only because of his honesty, integrity, and justness, but especially because of his simplicity and his learned ignorance.

Bridoye's trial is unquestionably humorous. Learned though he be, because he depends directly on divine Justice the judge appears foolish. The simplicity of his answers contrasts with the gravity of his situation. His defense has, moreover, a note of humor; for, although he appropriately cites Justinian law, he ironically juxtaposes the Latin legal corpus to the somewhat popular anecdotes that he relates. Through Bridoye Rabelais satirizes not only the language but also the wasteful practices of the legal profession of his day. He attacks the insistence on form that conceals the inanity of law and the greed of lawyers and judges. But the importance of his episode lies not so much in its attack on judicial materialism as in the revelation of the folly of Bridoye, which is humorously mundane and, at the same time, philosophical (*TL*/39–44).

Triboullet represents another aspect of folly and humor. Unlike Bridoye he is not well-educated. His is not the folly of learned ignorance, but of madness. Upon his arrival, Panurge presents Triboullet with a rattle made of an inflated pork bladder that contains peas, a gilded wooden sword, a tortoise-shell hunting pouch, a bottle of wine, and a quantity of apples. Triboullet girds on the sword, grasps the rattle, eats some of the apples, and drinks the bottle empty. Panurge, having taken particular note of the fool's last action, proceeds to set forth his case with great eloquence. Triboullet interrupts him. He gives Panurge a hearty slap on the chest, returns the bottle, and swats his nose with the bladder. Triboullet then goes apart from the group to listen to the rattle. He refuses further questioning; and when Panurge persists, Triboullet draws his "sword" to run him through.

Rabelais masterfully characterizes the essential differences and similarities between the folly of Bridoye and of Triboullet. Bridoye, like Rabelais, knows law. He is an educated man, a man of learning. He seems humorously foolish because of his simplicity, humility, and childlike trust in his fellow man and God. Though knowledgeable in the ways of the world he is not wise by worldly standards. On the contrary, although wise in the ways of God, he is a fool in man's eyes. Triboullet, by contrast, is mad. His actions are funny. Typically those of a court fool—childish, irrational—they evoke hearty laughter, not the benign smile occasioned by Bridoye's folly. Rabelais has no need of lengthy logical arguments to portray Triboullet. He speaks little; he has no interest in the company of the prince and his friends. Content to hear the rattle of beans in a bladder, like an infant, he is angered by any attempt to interrupt his peaceful play. He accepts the unreal for the real, mistaking a toy wooden sword for a weapon of steel. His is a world apart. In his folly and its cor-related symbolic drunkenness he attains the reality of divine inspiration.

In giving his interpretation of Triboullet's words and actions, Pantagruel first calls attention to the Dionysian aspect. He com-pares the shaking of the fool's head to the physical seizure of ancient oracles, divines, ecstatics, and the followers of Bacchus at the moment of inspiration. In interpreting Triboullet's words, he again makes reference to Panurge's *philautia,* but this time in terms of folly. Panurge foolishly wishes to marry at his age. He thinks that he himself is wise, but he is foolish through presumption. His folly is far more serious than Triboullet's madness. As usual, Pantagruel concludes that Panurge will be cuckolded. Moreover, Panurge will be beaten, as Triboullet signifies in swatting his nose. In response, Panurge as usual gives an opposing interpretation (*TL*/45–47).

Thus, the last of the consultations ends on the same tone of divergence as the others. Although Panurge's dilemma has not been resolved, he has achieved a certain amount of progress. He suggests the visit to the Dive Bouteille, and though he still looks to the Oracle as an outside source of truth, he will eventually achieve a certain kind of self-knowledge. The consultation with Triboullet has equally great significance in Rabelais's use of wine as symbol.

Neither Triboullet nor Bridoye attends the banquet, but they are an extension of its theme and an integral part of its inspiration. Bridoye represents the aspect of law and folly, Triboullet that of the Dionysian poetic furor. Thus, the *convivium* of the third book begins with a presentation of theological, medical, and philosophical wisdom, the highest human knowledge man can achieve about his soul and his body, and ends by looking forward to the learned ignorance of a judge and the Bacchic folly of a madman. Dialogue gives only a partial answer. One may learn through exterior means, but in the end, whether it be the dialogue of divination, of philosophy, or of folly, one must turn dialogue to self-reflection and contemplation. Rabelais, unlike Erasmus, does not clearly differentiate *wine* from *folly.* For him Bacchic furor and folly both symbolize the same divine inspiration.[22] But for the moment, the wisdom of wine leads only to the decision to seek truth from the Dive Bouteille. Thus the *Tiers Livre* concludes with a description of the preparation for the long voyage that begins and ends with Dionysian symbolism.

That voyage expresses most fully the meaning of wine as intuitive
dialectic.

3. *HOMO BIBENS:* CONTEMPLATIVE KNOWLEDGE
OF THE DIONYSIAN MYSTERIES

In the transformation of *homo ridens* to *homo bibens* at the end
of Book V, Rabelais gives the full significance of wine. For *homo
bibens* represents most completely the intuitive dialectic that
Rabelais expresses through the metaphorical voyage of the last
two books. That voyage and the visit to the oracle of the Dive
Bouteille at its conclusion adopt the wine symbolism of the
mysteries, which Rabelais suggests through imagery, ceremony,
and Bacchic furor.

The twelve ships of Pantagruel's fleet, as their ensigns show,
form a Dionysian thiasus, or ceremonial procession led by a bottle
and served by a lantern with ten Bacchantes as participants
(*QL/*1). The silver and carnation bottle ensign of the pilot ship,
reminiscent of the expression "être entre le blanc et le clairet" and
of the alchemically related metals silver and gold, suggests that
the voyage though subject to the inebriation of Bacchic inspiration
is controlled by reason.[23] The lantern of the intermediary second
vessel reminds the reader of Vergil's use of Venus to guide
Æneas from passion to reason and of the three lanterns who
show Dante the way to salvation in the *Commedia.*[24] The remaining ensigns display the finest assortment of drinking ware made
of the rarest metals or woods and crafted by the most delicate
workmanship.[25] Like the first two, they signify that Panurge's
voyage to self-discovery must lead through the world of shadow to
the folly of the Dive Bouteille.

Rabelais's Temple is extensively decorated with Bacchic symbols. The initiates gain entry only by passing through a vineyard
as eternally productive as the rejuvenation of the Dionysian mysteries. Similarly, they must walk under an archway that is

decorated with the representative wines, drinking vessels, and food of a Bacchic orgy. And they must pass beneath a trellised arbor cultivated from all imaginable species of vines and shaped by art (CL/34). The subterranean passageway leading from the trellis to the gateway bears frescos of a rustic dance of Corybantes and Satyrs accompanied by Silenus, laughing and mounted on his ass (CL/35). The main portal bears the motto "en vin verité," a reminder that the dialogic *conosce te ipsum* and the poetic furor of the Bacchic mysteries are one (CL/38).

Similarly, the ornamental vaulted ceiling of the Temple itself represents Bacchus' victory over the Indians (CL/39–40). In his description Rabelais transforms Lucian's short introductory study on Dionysos. He seizes with the sharp, clear, pictorial detail of the ancient *sarcophagi* the frenzy of Bacchus' army as they attack and totally rout the Indians who had disdainfully considered the god too effeminate to give them any worry.[26] This final allegorical symbol summarizes the entire myth of Dionysos. Through it Rabelais calls to mind the wild Bacchantes tearing Orpheus to shreds[27] as well as the spiritual and agrarian death and resurrection of Zagreus, Dionysos, and Osiris.[28] Through the folly of Dionysian mysteries Rabelais points to the interiorization of dialogue, but he uses external symbols and allegorical ceremonies to accomplish his purpose.

All the visitors to the Temple participate in the early stages of ceremonial initiation. While at the vineyard they eat three grapes each, place vine branches in their shoes, and take a green branch in their left hands. Before entering the vaulted archway they cover their heads with a "chapeau albanois," a kind of high-crowned hat woven from ivy branches. Their actions symbolize their willingness, as their Lanterne explains, to accept the Bacchic mysteries. They submit themselves in the manner of the ancient devotees of the cult to Dionysian furor, but only in subjection to symbolic inspiration and not to drunkenness. The ivy with which they cover their heads is a Bacchic symbol of constancy and represents the dominance of reason over passion in the pursuit of

Providential truth. Frère Jean confirms the symbolic meaning
of the ceremony by drawing an analogy with the Virgin of the
Apocalypse who stands on the moon (CL/34).[29] Once inside
the Temple itself they partake of a symbolic Dionysian feast.
At Bacbuc's bidding and through their imaginations they individually transform the water of the miraculous fountain into
wine and dine in sumptuous elegance from foods served by the
high priestess. In brief, they symbolically partake of truth; but
since this is Panurge's voyage of self-discovery it is left to him to
"drink" from the Dive Bouteille.

The final stages of initiatory ceremonies are appropriately
reserved for Panurge alone. Bacbuc takes him aside and admonishes him to listen to the Bottle with one ear, that is, atten-
tively. She dresses him in a "galleverdine," a kind of long, smock-
like over garment of coarse material; covers his head with a white
"beguin," a nun's hood; gives him "une chausse d'hypocras," a
penitential garment, as breeches; covers his hands with old
codpieces as gloves; and gives him three bag pipes tied together
as a belt. The ritual begins. Bacbuc bathes Panurge's face three
times in the fountain and then throws flour in his face. She
places three cock feathers on the right side of the breeches, makes
him walk around the fountain nine times, jump up in the air
three times, and sit down on the ground seven times. The entire
ceremony is accompanied by conjurations in Etruscan and read-
ings from a book of ritual carried by one of Bacbuc's attendant
mystagogues.

In addition to the apparent satire of ceremony and ritual,
Rabelais suggests a symbolic meaning in these rites. Through
their association with the Etruscan language, the rituals take on
the character of Bacchic ceremonies of purification. But Rabelais
extends their meaning to include, by association, all the ancient
Roman, Etruscan, Hebrew, Egyptian, and Attic mysteries. They
are, therefore, universal symbols of purification, as further suggested by the constant use of the numbers *three, nine,* and *seven.*
The numbers *three* and *nine* indicate the triple aspects of God

and man in the Neoplatonic and related Cabalistic and Christian traditions. *Seven,* also a universal symbol, calls to mind the astrological fountain and suggests the Orphic aspect of the Dionysian cults (*CL*/42). Rabelais perhaps had this association in mind when referring to the harmony of the fountain, for Orpheus' lyre is a symbol of the harmony of the spheres. Orpheus is, moreover, the high priest of Bacchus. Through his own descent into hell he reminds us that the equivalent mysteries of Dionysos and Osiris are symbolically mysteries of spiritual purification. To those traditions of antiquity Rabelais also adds the ancient Cabalistic equation of wine and mystery, an association suggested by the use of the Hebrew word for bottle, *Bacbuc,* as the name for the high priestess of the Dive Bouteille.[30] All of these mysteries are dualistic and have in common the need for purification of the body. Although Rabelais, as has been seen, gives a positive value to the corporal element of man, he too sees the need for recognition of the body as shadow. Man must rise above the earth in order to see Truth. In Panurge's case the *braguettes* and *cornemeuses* suggest the specific nature of purification required. Panurge must rid himself of a dominant sensual appetite before he can achieve self-knowledge. Panurge symbolically enacts this purification through the ceremonies he performs; but especially by sitting down seven times, he signifies the need to dominate his lower nature. These rites of purification are also a symbolic initiation into the mysteries of the Dive Bouteille.

Bacbuc leads Panurge into the holy of holies, a perfectly spherical chapel apart from the Temple proper. The shape of the chapel that houses the Bottle would indicate that Panurge has arrived at the highest point of his journey to the world of Ideas and that the journey must be interiorized in terms of the descent-ascent motif. But Panurge must first appeal to the Oracle externally. He performs additional rites suggestive of the Bacchic cults of initiation and then he chants a Dionysian ἐπιλήνιος. His incantatory poem of praise to Bacchus forms the visual image of a bottle in the manner of the *technopaegnia* of classical antiquity and the *carmina figurata* of the Latin Christian era.[31] Imitating the form of the bucolic figure poems practiced by his contemporaries Stephen Hawes, Salmonius Macrinus, and Melin de Saint-Gelais, among others,[32] and perhaps following the example of the Dionysian furor of the Pléiade,[33] Rabelais has Panurge sing a harvest song of praise to the god of wine. Without realizing that he has done so, Panurge has already expressed through that poem the idea of temperance which serves as the solution to his own problem. But he must first transform the oracular "TRINCH" of the Bottle into a personalized experience through poetic furor.

It is fitting and necessary that Panurge find his own answer. The dialogues of divination, of philosophy, and of folly in Book III have pointed the way to self-knowledge. During the voyage of self-discovery Panurge has been accompanied by a guide. The mediatory second ship symbolizes in general the principle of the Lanterne and represents more concretely the companionly guidance given by Pantagruel and his friends. The last step of the journey after the realm of Quinte Essence from Lantern Land to the gate of the Temple is watched over by the Lanterne who was in life the mistress of Rabelais's platonizing friend Pierre Lamy (*CL*/33-37).[34] But much as Vergil and Beatrice must leave Dante as he passes, respectively, under the influence of Revelation and Divine Light,[35] so Panurge's Lanterne can only lead him to the realm of Ideas. Just as Bernard can only point the way for Dante, whose beatific vision is his own,[36] so Bacbuc can only lead Panurge to the oracle. His interpretation of it must be his own. He must literally incorporate it within himself, for the world of Ideas exists within the individual. To suggest the process of interiorization Rabelais resorts to poetic furor.

Rabelais makes no clear distinction among the four Platonic furors. Apollonian prophecy, Dionysian mysteries, the poetry of the Muses, and the philosophical furor of celestial Love show in his work the interrelation that Plato ascribes to them in the *Phaedrus* and that they were given in the mythological traditions

of antiquity.[37] Unlike Tyard and Ficino, Rabelais offers no clearly
defined hierarchical pattern with ascendent degrees, for example,
poetry, mysteries, prophecy, and Love.[38] It would seem that
Ficino himself was never certain about the relative ranks the
several furors should hold: for he, while retaining a hierarchical
pattern, altered their positions at various times.[39] Rabelais is in
agreement, however, with Ficino in insisting on the interiority of
furor and in showing a progressive development from nature to
opinion to discursive reason and to angelic intellect or the philosophical dialectic in terms of self-knowledge. But he does not
associate this progress with specific furors. He rather presents
the several forms of inspiration compositely as folly and Bacchic
furor.

Rabelais may not conceive of furor in a hierarchical pattern,
but he does associate it with a transformation. At the level of
imagery, as Bacbuc points out, furor symbolizes interiorization
of dialogue, which Rabelais represents by the metamorphosis
from *homo ridens* to *homo bibens:*

> Et icy maintenons que non rire, ains boire est le propre
> de l'homme; je ne dy boire simplement et absolument, car
> aussi bien boivent les bestes: je dis boire vin bon et frais.
> Notez, amis, que de vin divin on devient, et n'y a argu-
> ment tant seur, ny art de divination moins fallace. (*CL*/45).

In the context Bacbuc recalls the Socratic *conosce te ipsum* within
a framework of Rabelaisian *caritas*. Thus Rabelais's *homo bibens*
symbolizes the interior dialogue of intuitive self-knowledge. That
Panurge attains that state is seen in a transformation of the
Dionysian mode to the Apollonian.

"Io Pean, Io Pean, Io Pean!" Panurge is exultant. He has
overcome his fear, and he expresses his joy through the traditional
cry of joy and victory addressed to Apollo who succeeded Pæan
as physician to the gods. His threefold repetition of "Io Pean"
implies victory over past fears and evil, joy in the present for
being healed, and for the future an omen of success in marriage
when coupled with "Io mariage trois fois." This cry of joy serves

as the key to the entire quest and voyage. All of the consultations and experience of three books are summed up in Panurge's chant of exultation. Rabelais could have chosen no better way to express Panurge's finding self-knowledge, his overcoming his fears, his conquering *philautia* and restoring harmony than by adapting from Plutarch's *De E apud Delphos* the intrinsic meaning of this shout of victory to the god of light. Dionysos is transformed into Apollo; winter has become spring, death life, the dithyramb the paean; disorder has given way to harmony, passion to reason. Panurge is healed, he is whole again.[40] Yet, because his language retains its basic sensuality, Rabelais apparently does not intend this experience as a miraculous metamorphosis. It is a *conversion,* a turning inward, through and with divine inspiration. It is self-knowledge, which is clearly not the same for Panurge, for Pantagruel, and for Frère Jean. Their three examples of Bacchic enthusiasm portray, in fact, three different modes of knowledge.

Panurge, whose dilemma remains the central issue, continues to function at a very basic, physical level. His Bacchic seizure, nevertheless, leads him to prophesy. Looking into the future, made certain only through self-knowledge, he sees in the present his acts of physical love. Then, as though questioning himself for the first time, he sees in his heart with certainty that he will be married and that his wife will gladly join him in the sexual act. Thus, his twofold question is answered. *He* answers it. He will be married. He will not be cuckolded, for his wife will not find him too old and she will not seek physical satisfaction elsewhere. Moreover, since he now has restored harmony within himself, she will reflect that order. Panurge's interest in marriage remains the satisfaction of physical pleasure. He envisions his success as a "debat," but a friendly, mutually agreeable tussle in which he will be satisfied. And, in a sense, he now applies Rondibilis' advice. He will overcome desire through the acceptable means of matrimony. He will be not only a satisfied husband but a good one. Panurge thus has reason to shout with joy, "Io Pean!" At length he finds, within himself, an oracle that he can accept without question, an oracle that by definition is *fatidique*. He controls through self-knowledge and free will his actions, and since he now wills to marry, that decision is certain. He can now turn to his friend Frère Jean and invite him to share his joy and newfound knowledge.

Frère Jean, however, does not seem indulgent toward Panurge. To the contrary, he appears skeptical. At most he thinks Panurge has gone mad or that he is under a spell. Frère Jean seeks an explanation to which the rationality of his faith leads him. He wonders how far Panurge's seeming madness will go, what medical remedy Panurge will take to effect his own cure, or if he will follow the popular superstition and take a hair from the mad dog that caused his mental derangement. Frère Jean mocks Panurge, and when he too is apparently seized by poetic furor, his language remains playful and rationally skeptical.

Pantagruel, on the other hand, understands Panurge's actions. He too rhymes; but he transcends the level of passion demonstrated by Panurge and that of rational skepticism of Frère Jean. The first three decasyllables of Pantagruel's poem state immediately the nature of Panurge's seizure. Panurge is overcome by the poetic furor of Bacchus. Consequently he becomes an oracle, voicing the will of God manifested providentially in the zodiacal *Eclipticus* of which wine is another symbol. Pantagruel then sets forth the effects of this divine inspiration on Panurge. Overcome by the higher force, Panurge progresses from "cris," the misery of uncertainty, to joy, manifested by "ris," and the certainty of decision, "pris." He, as poet of the gods, conquers the doubting smiles of his friends, although in this manifestation of furor he is equally the king of fools. Pantagruel recognizes the symbolic importance of Panurge's seizure as well as his moral progress. He sees no reason for mocking him, as Frère Jean has done. Pantagruel's language is philosophical. The form of his verse is symmetrical, the last three decasyllables repeating the pattern of the first three. He *logically* expresses the signifi-

cance of poetic furor. But, through his use of verse, he also
shows that his knowledge, like that of Socrates, transcends the
plane of discursive reason. In poetizing, he represents the ideal
Sage who, unlike the Stoic sage satirized by Erasmus, does not
found his wisdom on human knowledge alone but in intuitive
dialectic (*CL*/46).

Panurge resumes his poetizing in a more elevated tone. He
leaves aside his concern for marriage and cuckoldry. Having resolved those problems, he now underlines the principal theme
of the quest, the significance of the Dive Bouteille as a symbol of
the Socratic *conosce te ipsum*. The oracle of the Bottle is certain
as any of those rendered by the Pythian Oracle at Delphi. If
Plutarch had drunk from its fountain, he would not have won-
dered why the oracles had ceased, for he would know that the
only sure art of divination was that of the "TRINCH." Rabelais,
thus, appropriately leaves the final explanation of the oracle to
Panurge. In showing its significance through poetic furor,
Panurge manifests definite understanding of his new knowledge.
He is so certain of the answer he has attained that he again invites Frère Jean to ask the oracle if he should marry or not.
Frère Jean, however, finds Panurge's solution appropriate to
Panurge. But he takes his own vows seriously, and the *fureur*
with which he replies to Panurge's suggestion is as much
anger as furor. Panurge takes off his mystical garb, and Frère
Jean brings the furor to an end by proposing that they settle their
dispute in conviviality by drinking together.

The episode of the Dive Bouteille shows the full significance
of the *convivium* in Rabelais's thought. Bacchic furor is a composite symbol, including the several forms of divine inspiration
represented by poetic furor, vaticination or oracular divination,
the initiatory mysteries, and the philosophical furor itself. Pantagruel, Frère Jean, and Panurge through the medium of wine are
overcome by divine inspiration. Through their poetic furor
Rabelais shows the insufficiency of human reason and man's need
to seek divine will in his individual life. At the same time, how-

ever, he points to the necessity of the threefold nature of man; the nonrational, rational, and intuitive aspects represented, respectively, by Panurge, Frère Jean, and Pantagruel. As though applying Plutarch's idea that the gods give the inspiration but not the words, rhymes, or metre to the sibyls, Rabelais presents the three levels of human nature in the poetizing of his three characters.[41] None of the levels is sufficient, however, in itself; and each of the characters, while still portraying a basic type of intellect, participates through his poetizing in all three. Thus, Rabelais reiterates the lesson of the *convivium* and the chapters on education in the earlier books. Human sciences are necessary for man in his search for knowledge. But like the irrationality of emotions and like the discursive reason on which they are based, the sciences are insufficient. This conclusion has been seen in the episodes of Bridoye and Triboullet, but Panurge's consultation with the fool and the lesson he might have learned from the discussion about Bridoye do not have the meaning for him that the "TRINCH" has. For these examples, like those of the divinatory consultations and the advice of the guests at the *convivium*, remain exterior. Only in seeking truth within himself can he resolve his problems and doubts and calm his fears. Bacchic furor and the voyage theme thus clearly have a dialogic signification for Rabelais. Just as poetic furor symbolizes self-knowledge, so the initiatory rites of the Bacchic mysteries signify the correlated purification of the philosophical dialectic.

For Rabelais, as for other Renaissance Platonists, the initiatory rites of religious experience symbolize philosophical purification. This is the meaning he gives to the Dionysiac rites in which Pantagruel and his companions participate. Panurge is purified from terrestrial stain by turning into himself and by reestablishing the proper balance between will and reason, on the one hand, and physical passion on the other. Rabelais certainly does not, however, imply a rejection of religious values. Nor does he consider the "ability to rage correctly" purely metaphorical as Plato seems to have done.[42] Rabelais, a Renaissance Platonist, conceives of the mystery rites as a symbolic expression of the highest wisdom of which *homo bibens* is capable.

Each of the three aspects of Rabelaisian wine symbolism has its own intrinsic value in the dialogic experience. The conviviality of *homo ridens* embodies the principles of man at play and the literal level of friendly conversational exchange of social man. The charitable attitude that pervades conviviality is necessary for the intellectual exchange of ideas of the philosophical dialogue. The three external modes of consultation through divination, philosophical intercourse, and folly serve as sound means of acquiring truth, but they must give way to the interiorized intuitive dialectic of *homo bibens* who symbolizes the complete man. He functions at all three levels of dialogue. But only through his transformation of externally acquired truth into an individual intuitive experience can he acquire self-knowledge, knowledge of God, knowledge of fellow man, and knowledge of the world around him.

In this exploration of the Rabelaisian dialectic, man's relationship to the world has only been touched upon. The study of the Platonic basis of dialogue has led to a consideration of the ideal nature of man and his knowledge. That study has to a very great extent led away from the tangible world of empirical experience. In the third chapter the dialogue will be examined as a link between the ideal and physical levels of reality through an investigation of the hermetic sciences in Rabelais's literary work.

NOTES

1. Léon Robin, "Notice," in Platon, *Le Banquet, Œuvres complètes,* t. IV, 2, xii–xvii. Similar Renaissance adaptations of the *symposion* may be seen in Ficino's commentary and Castiglione's *Courtier.* In Rabelais's *convivium* the first speaker Hippothadée begins immediately after the second course, always served with claret. Rondibilis, judging from Panurge's reference to a "pasté de coins," a pâté served at dessert, is still speaking at the conclusion of the meal. The third speaker, the philosopher Trouillogan, apparently takes the floor after dinner (*TL,* Ch. 30). *Cf.* Sainéan, *Langue de Rabelais,* I, 171–89.

2. "Hic medicae fons est exundatissimus artis. Hinc, mage ni sapiat pigra lacuna, bibe": *Œuvres,* ed. Marty-Laveaux, t. III, 315, and *cf.* "Commentaire," t. IV, 376.

3. The legendary origin of Pantagruel and other specific examples of its use by Rabelais are discussed by Lefranc, "Introduction," *Pantagruel,* t. III, xiv–xxiv.

4. *Symposium,* 212c–223a.

5. Water is the image implicit in the epigram of the Hippocrates edition. Water, normally associated with the *fons cabalin,* becomes "nectar divin, vin precieux . . ." in the "Prologue" to Book V (Plattard, V, 5–6). For a fuller discussion of the meaning of nectar, see Leo Hebraeus, *Dialoghi,* III, ed. Gebhardt, foll. 52vo–55ro, and *De l'amour,* trans. Tyard, t. II, 143–53. See also Evelyn Underhill, *Mysticism: A Study in the Nature and Development of Man's Spiritual Consciousness,* pp. 235–37, 278. The language of Rabelais's passage quoted in the text above leaves no doubt about Rabelais's dialogic adaptation of the *fons.*

6. See Underhill, *Mysticism,* pp. 235–36.

7. *Phaedrus,* 244d–245a, 265a/c.

8. Thomas à Kempis, *De imitatione Christi,* IV, x.

9. Santa Teresa, *The Life,* trans. J. M. Cohen, Ch. 18, pp. 126, *et passim.* For additional examples, see Underhill, *Mysticism,* pp. 236–41. See also Dante, *Paradiso,* IV, 114–17, and Thenaud, *Traité de poesie,* B. N., Ms. fr. 2081, fol. 1ro, for examples, respectively, of the images "Fountain of Life" and "Fonteine de vie."

10. *Gargantua,* t. I, 52–66, nn. 1, 22.

11. Lefranc, "Le vin chez Rabelais," *RSS,* XI (1924), 65. Similar

examples of the companionly dialogue of conviviality are seen in *G*, Chs. 39–41 and *QL*, Chs. 53–55.

12. Plato, *Laws*, I–II, 634b–649b, 663b–674c.

13. A detailed analysis of the consultations and the symposium is given by Screech, *Rabelaisian Marriage*, pp. 66–103.

14. *Cf. Republic*, IX, 580d–581c and *Laws*, V, 726a–734e.

15. *Cf.* Cassirer, *The Individual and the Cosmos*, pp. 21–23.

16. Verdun L. Saulnier, *Le dessein de Rabelais*, pp. 63–66. See also Walter Jacob Kaiser, *Praisers of Folly: Erasmus, Rabelais, Shakespeare*, pp. 103–110; and Screech, *Rabelaisian Marriage*, pp. 104–125. See also Enzo Nardi, *Rabelais e il diritto romano*, pp. 131–218.

17. See Jean Plattard, *L'Invention et la composition dans l'œuvre de Rabelais*, pp. 315–17.

18. Desiderius Erasmus, *Moriae encomium*, pp. 60–62. Marcel Tetel, *Etude sur le comique de Rabelais*, p. 103, discusses the *comic* aspects of Triboullet's *blason*.

19. See, for example, Kaiser, *Praisers of Folly*, pp. 173–74.

20. Agrippa, "Ad lectorem," *De incertitudine et vanitate scientiarum atque artium*, *Opera*, II, foll. 4ʳᵒ–6ʳᵒ; also *Declamation sur l'incertitude, vanité et abus des sciences*, trans. Louis de Mayerne-Turquet, foll. 2ʳᵒ–6ʳᵒ.

21. *Symposium*, 201d–212c.

22. Erasmus, *Moriae encomium*, pp. 107–13.

23. Although I have found no explanation for the origin of this expression, it may well have arisen from the habit of beginning a meal with white wine and serving claret with the second and remaining courses, dessert being accompanied by a red wine. See Sainéan, *Langue de Rabelais*, I, 171–89; Huguet, II, 304; Littré (1885), IV, 2495.

24. For the allegorical interpretation of Vergil, see Christophoro Landino, *Disputationes Camaldulenses* in *Chriſtophori Landini Florentini Libri Quattuor*, sig. F–iiiʳᵒ–F–iiijᵛᵒ.

25. See L. Denoix, "Les Connaissances nautiques de Rabelais," in *François Rabelais: Ouvrage publié pour le quatrième centenaire de sa mort*, pp. 172–73.

26. See Lucian, "Dionysus, An Introduction," trans. A. M. Harmon, I, 47–59, and "Praefatio, seu Bacchus," *Opera*, III, 74–85; *CL*/39, ed. Plattard, n.1, p. 341; and Martin P. Nilsson, *The Dionysiac Myſteries of the Helleniſtic and Roman Age*, pp. 61, 116–31.

27. Lucian, *Opera*, II, 77; Euripides, *Bacchanals*, vv. 677–774.

28. *Cf.* Nilsson, *Dionysiac Mysteries*, pp. 38–43, 116–31, and André Boulanger, *Orphée: Rapports de l'orphisme et du christianisme*, pp. 23–27.

29. Apocalypsis 12:1: *Et signum magnum apparuit in caelo: mulier amicta sole, et luna sub pedibus eius, et in capite eius corona stellarum duodecim.* A similar reference may be seen in the Tarot. See J. E. Cirlot, *A Dictionary of Symbols*, pp. 204–207, 310–12, and Arthur Edward Waite, *The Pictorial Key to the Tarot*, pp. 76–79, 283.

30. *Cf.* Robert Ambelain, *La Kabbale pratique*, p. 26. Rabelais, "Briefve declaration: Bacbuc," *Quart Livre*, ed. Plattard, IV, 249; ed. Boulenger, p. 761.

31. A rather exhaustive bibliography of texts and criticism for the *technopaegnia* and *carmina figurata* is given in my study, "Rabelais and Renaissance Figure Poems," *Etudes rabelaisiennes*, VIII, 39–54. See also Weinberg, "Rabelais and Christian Hermetism," who has identified Pantagruel's poem (*CL/46*) as a chalice, pp. 95–103.

32. See Margaret Church, "The First English Pattern Poems," *PMLA*, LXI (1946), 636–50; James Hutton, *The Greek Anthology in France, and in the Latin Writers of the Netherlands to the Year 1800*, pp. 782–83; and *The Greek Anthology in Italy to the Year 1800*, p. 624. Additional bibliography is given in my article cited above, n. 31.

33. See A. Desguine, *Arcueil et les poètes du XVIᵉ siècle*, pp. 34–35.

34. Rabelais, ed. Plattard, V, 134, and n. 19.

35. Dante, *Purgatorio*, I, and *Paradiso*, XXX, and Charles S. Singleton, *Journey to Beatrice, Dante Studies 2*, especially pp. 57–71.

36. Dante, *Paradiso*, XXXI–XXXIII.

37. *Phaedrus*, 244d–245a, 265a/c.

38. Ficino, *Commentaire sur le Banquet*, VII, xiii, xiv, ed. Marcel, pp. 257–60. Pontus de Tyard, *Le Solitaire premier, Œuvres*, ed. Silvio F. Baridon, pp. 17–20.

39. André Chastel, *Marsile Ficin et l'art*, pp. 129–33. For variants in the hierarchical pattern, *cf.* Ficino, *Opera omnia*, I, 614–15, II, 1365.

40. Plutarch, *Moralia*, 388e–389c.

41. Plutarch, *Moralia*, 397b/c.

42. Wind, *Pagan Mysteries*, pp. 13–23.

abelais had no need to reconcile Nature and the Ideal. For him, as for the Florentine Platonists, Aristotelian empiricism and Platonic intuition were complementary extremes of the dialectic of opposites.[1] God, who reconciles all antitheses, reflects himself in the ideal and in the natural. He transcends both and is immanent in both. And man also participates in the two aspects of divine creation. As an image of the divine, man partakes partially of angelic intuition. As a creature, his most natural means to knowledge is through sensory perception. Thus, though man's grasp of it is limited, the world of empirical fact is a very necessary part of his dialogic experience.[2]

Although Rabelais regards the teacher of Alexander as the most notable philosopher of his own day (*G*/14, *TL*/Prol.), Aristotle remains above all a naturalist for him. Rabelais cites him in matters pertaining to mathematics and logic.[3] But the learned philosopher appears most often in his work in humorous or straightforward references to medicine and, in general, to the nature of the world and its creatures.[4] As the allegory of the Pays de Satin suggests, Aristotle holds a lantern to light the way for naturalists (*CL*/31). But the food he and his imitators in the land of Ouy-dire offer Rabelais's voyagers is not sufficient (*CL*/32), and so they move on to the land of Lanterns and the metaphysical truth of the Dive Bouteille. They find the natural philosophy of Aristotle a necessary complement to the dialectical truth of the *Platonici;* within itself, however, it is incomplete. Though they might find in the *livres de prime philosophie* attributed to Aristotle an essential expression of the Hermetic sciences, they would insist equally on the speculative as well as the empirical aspects of those sciences.[5]

More than any other feature of Renaissance thought reflected in Rabelais's literary work the Hermetic sciences of astrology, alchemy, magic, and the Cabala point to the oneness of the empirical and idealistic tendencies of the Platonic-Hermetic tradition. Those several sciences as developed in the late Hellenistic and Christian eras all share a common origin in both Aristotelian and Neoplatonic sources.[6] In fact, the sources are inseparable inasmuch as the Renaissance not only interpreted the Aristotelian corpus in the light of the speculative traditions but also thought it to contain authentic documents on the occult sciences. Rabelais was certainly aware of such patterns of interrelation. They should be borne in mind in this dialectic consideration of the Hermetic sciences in the perspective of Nature, as occult sciences of superstition, as empirical disciplines, and as metaphysical speculations.

1. PHYSIS AND THE HERMETIC SCIENCES

The many references to Nature and *le naturel* in Rabelais have led some critics to see him unqualifiedly as a hedonist.[7] But a careful evaluation of Nature in his work will show the inseparableness of the concept from harmony, reason, and moderation. The orderliness of Nature closely parallels the logical processes of human thinking based on sensory perception. Both reflect the divine plan that makes itself manifest in the inner workings of natural law and in the "occult" forces of Nature.

Rabelais's adaptation of Calcagnini's fable of Physis and Antiphysie leaves no doubt that harmony is the prime characteristic he gives Nature the creative agent $(QL/32)$.[8] Her children are essentially beautiful, while those of Antiphysie are monstrous inversions. In sharp antithesis to the Platonic tree, their heads are diabolically turned downward and away from their divine origin.[9] As their names suggest, the children of Antiphysie, Amodunt and Discordance, personify the excess and discord Panurge sees in the world without debts $(TL/3-4)$. For Rabelais, however, Antiphysie represents an inversion of total universal order. Indirectly through his inversion Panurge gives expression to that order; and Rabelais describes it positively in the mystical fountain.

The fountain of the Temple de la Dive Bouteille ($CL/42$), which Rabelais borrowed from Colonna's *Hypnerotomachia Poliphili*,[10] compositely symbolizes the ordered universe. The crystal cupola that surmounts the whole structure calls to mind the Emperean sphere and the *Anima Mundi*. Its inscriptions signify the *primum mobile* that in Aristotelian and Platonic cosmogony gives the first impulse of the movement of divine order to the sphere of the fixed stars or Zodiac. The seven planetary spheres then continue the movement in the pattern Rabelais believed first described by Chaldean and Egyptian *magi*.[11] The perfect order of the ten spheres reflects the perfection of divine will and ideal form in the temporal cycles of years, seasons, months, and days. But that perfection of the celestial world gives way to change in the elemental world of sublunar influence.

The four hierarchically disposed elements of fire, air, water, and earth compose all matter. Though created from the perfect quintessence of the heavenly spheres, the elements are by nature corrupt. When the vital force that gives them form expires, they return to their natural position. The elements thus give the impression of being constantly at war ($TL/3$).[12] Yet within Rabelais's conception of their role they participate in the pattern of orderliness because they give substance to the members of species; although individuals must die the species themselves are immortal. They participate in a hierarchical pattern ordered by natural law. Each individual member, as well as each species in the descending hierarchy, has its own essential nature that reflects the perfection of the ideal realm of divine intelligence.[13] They thus form a chain of being in which each greater entity subsumes the next lower entity within an overall pattern of the One, Intellect (Angel), Soul (Man), Sense (Animal), Being (Vegetable).[14] Through that hierarchical relationship the celestial and earthly worlds of Nature are sympathetically related. Rabelais's fountain suggests that the constellations and planets influence not only physical objects and lower species but also man's body.

The fountain of Rabelais's Temple has as its conceptual basis the idea of a sympathetic relationship among the gods or daimons believed to animate the seven planets, the planets themselves, and the metals, gems, animals, and birds of the "geocosm." [15] As Panurge suggests, the planets and stars of the Zodiac, moreover, have a strong influence on the organs and parts of the microcosm $(TL/4)$.[16] Thus man has a medicinal interest in rediscovering the natural sympathetic ties, for through them he can treat his own maladies or bodily "disorders." [17] As a naturally curious creature $(CL/47)$,[18] he turns to the world around him for information and power. Through a study of the movements of the planets and stars he finds not only an expression of order but also a plan that could potentially affect his own life. And through judicial astrology he would hope to discover the future. In the quintessential relationship between the celestial world and metals, gems, and plants the alchemist seeks to discover the nature of the transmutation of elements and perhaps the secret of making gold or of life itself. The magus investigates the affinity among objects and tries to control them and natural forces through his knowledge of the laws of Nature. The Cabalist practices all those arts and/or studies in philosophical speculation the nature and power of the sacred word and letter in a tradition that he believed was first revealed to Adam.[19]

Whichever of the sciences his curiosity may follow, the natural philosopher has before him three possible paths to knowledge. If he practices the black arts through an attempt to manipulate demonic forces or if he superstitiously pursues magical divination or judicial astrology, the naturalist follows the path of the occultist. His safest way is that of the empiricist who seeks in Nature knowledge of the orderly laws of creation, of himself, and of his Creator. But in his investigation of the Hermetic sciences the natural philosopher may indeed find the path to the speculative, metaphysical traditions of the Cabala and the initiatory mysteries of Hermetism.

2. THE BLACK ARTS:
VANITY, ABUSE, AND SUPERSTITION

Rabelais's reader quickly becomes aware of the scorn in which he held the black arts. His condemnation of judicial astrology and the alchemical "art de Lullius" (*P*/8) seems to contradict, however, his positive emphasis on the supernatural presages of comets and elemental disturbances that announced the death of Guillaume Du Bellay (*QL*/25–27).[20] But behind the satire of astrologers, alchemists, magicians, and practical cabalists, the careful reader finds a straightforward acceptance of the natural basis for those arts.

Nowhere does Rabelais give a more direct statement on judicial astrology than in his satirical almanacs. His *Pantagrueline prognostication certaine, veritable pour l'an perpetuel*[21] underlines the essential vanity of astrologers who take advantage of the credulity and curiosity of the people. So strong is Rabelais's opposition to astrologers that he insists on the need for censorship to check their abuses of the simple and ignorant. But his main criticism stems from their substitution of a secondary force for the prime causal agent.

God moves all things in the universe. All life depends on Him and on His will as Creator. But the *folz astrologues* would transform the stars, which are nothing more than signs or at the most secondary and intermediate causes in the phenomenal world, into primary influences.[22] Although Rabelais sees the heavenly bodies as means of revealing divine will, he states clearly in his *Almanach de 1533* that man should not endeavor to read in them or into them the "secrets du conseil estroit du Roy eternel."[23] And in the *Almanach de 1535* he comes to the heart of the matter in showing that man's powers of observation are insufficient to measure with accuracy celestial movements.[24] Although man's body remains subject to the stars his situation is not entirely pessimistic; for man's will is not subject to sidereal influence, and through harmonizing human will with divine will man can transcend unfavorable astral contingencies. But he must avoid the practice of the astrologers who seek to impose their will on the heavens. Their attempt to control the constellations and planets inverts the natural order of knowledge and is the prime source of their abuses and vanities.[25] They share that dialogic inversion with alchemists and magicians.

Through the language of alchemy in parody and satire Rabelais indirectly condemns those alchemists who abuse their knowledge through an inversion of its application. For example, in depicting Panurge's use of a "philosopher's stone" to steal money from the indulgence banks in Paris, Rabelais playfully attacks Panurge's method of curing his malady "faulte d'argent." But at the same time he attacks the inanity of a search for the philosopher's stone and the gullibility of those who believe a stone can attract gold ($P/17$). Rabelais gives a similar example in the episode of the Papimanes where gold is drawn with alchemical subtlety from France to Rome through the use of decretals ($QL/53$).

By far the most extensive adaptation of alchemical symbolism is seen in the visit to the Chats fourrez. In his alchemical parody of the Chats fourrez Rabelais attacks the very basis of the judicial system in France. The Chats, who represent judges, generally control their victims through *la sexte essence*. They surpass the quintessence of the alchemists, for their claws of injustice are a much surer means of extracting gold. The litany in which their chief justice Grippeminault participates shows the three stages of the "sextessential" process. With a curt "or ça" the judge admonishes the individuals before him to direct their attention to the matter at hand; and he suggests that their guilt or innocence depends on gold. In the second phase of interchange Panurge forcefully answers with an "or là," ostensibly throwing his purse of gold "LÀ" before the judge. Finally Grippeminault resolves the case and assures his innocent victims of their acquittal by an "or bien" (CL/11-13). His final cry of satisfaction condemns the Chats fourrez just as the black weevil of Grippeminault's enigma condemns itself by devouring the white bean that shelters it.

The Great Work of the alchemists has a philosophical as well as a practical end. Philosophical alchemy, regarded as the true science by its adepts, is speculative and symbolic. Totally divorced from the search for gold, speculative alchemy gives the philosopher's stone or gold a spiritual meaning. Thus the transformation of metals signifies regeneration, not of metals, but of the soul. The colors associated with the transmutation in the alchemist's furnace or egg designate the several stages in spiritual development. The alchemical process begins with a black *materia prima* that is followed in turn by union and putrefaction or death. The spiritual death is succeeded by a purificatory process of washing, which produces whiteness. This stage is, however, intermediary and is followed by a third transformation (reddening) and possibly, though not necessarily, by a fourth (yellowness).[26] But the Chats fourrez reverse this process. They are red with the blood of their victims in this life and become black beetles or vipers in the next. Instead of being reborn white or pure from the blackness of corruption, they are born black from the white bean or egg (CL/14). Thus, by seemingly exceeding the quintessence of alchemy, they bring about their own ruin through their sextessential corruption. They transform knowledge and power for good into evil as black and diabolic as any practiced in demonic magic.

By a series of puns and mistaken identities Rabelais turns Gymnaste's encounter with Tripet and his men into a satire of the popular beliefs and superstitious practices of demonic magic (G/34-35). Picrochole's unreasonable men endow Gymnaste, who introduces himself as a "pauvre diable," with all the powers a devil should have. They go so far as to exorcize him, and in the end their irrational fear causes them to be completely routed by Gymnaste's acrobatic stunts. So quickly does fear spread among them that before their next sortie they all cross themselves with holy water and wear a star-shaped amulet to protect themselves from the diabolic influence of Gargantua's forces. Superstitious "faith" in the magical efficacy of the pentagram can not, however, protect the Picrocholine hordes from the superior reason and justness of their opponents before whom they flee in panic ($G/43$). Their unreasonable actions reflect on a popular level the learned practice of magic by Her Trippa.

Rabelais leaves no doubt about his condemnation of Trippa's black magic ($TL/25$). If the omission of Pantagruel from the visit and Panurge's own unusually violent reaction at the end of the episode were not sufficient signs, the wolfskin and sword presented to Trippa as gifts in exchange for his advice symbolize the demonic nature of his art.[27] By no means do all his methods of divination suggest sorcery, but they are all closely associated with charlatanism. Necromancy, the last art on his list, clearly points to his infernal interests. Several of the methods he mentions earlier depend upon the evocation of either dead souls or, in Panurge's case, living images of his future wife. In both instances, however, there is some question among Christian authorities whether it is the actual spirit of the person evoked who appears or a demon that bears his form. By hydromancy and lecanomancy, for example, the magician calls forth the image of a person respectively in a stream or fountain or in a basin of water. For these methods, as well as for those which depend on mirrors, sieves, cheese, incense, or wax, among others enumerated by Her Trippa, the magus must make elaborate preparations and perform suitable rites. But although Rabelais like other humanists shows interest in these arts of divination he was surely aware as were his classical antecedents of the charlatanism practiced through them.[28] Though he accepts the philosophical basis for these and all other so-called occult sciences, he clearly condemns them as abuses and black arts.

Just as Rabelais satirizes the "occult" applications of astrology, alchemy, and magic, so he satirizes the practical cabala, which he relates to those superstitious sciences ($P/20$).[29] He attacks the "cabalistes de Sainlouand," whom he associates with popular cabalistic traditions of diabolic exorcism (*G*/8, 35) and with the *cabale monastique*. This latter *cabale monastique* inverts, therefore, the religious practices associated with the metaphysical speculations of the Cabala.

Rabelais criticizes the black arts because they indeed invert the natural order of knowledge. Man is endowed with an innate curiosity to learn. So long as he investigates Nature and uses his knowledge of natural laws and forces, he turns away from his initial and ultimate divine source. He inverts human reason and through excess destroys the balance within himself and his relationship to the world.

3. EMPIRICISM AND THE LIMITS OF HUMAN REASON

Behind each of the occult sciences of the Renaissance lies an empirical discipline of which the black art is an inversion. In Rabelais's thought, astrology, for example, depends on astronomy, the scientific observation of heavenly bodies. Alchemy has its basis in an orderly investigation of the properties of metals, gems, stones, and herbs. And the related science of magic expresses logical knowledge of the forces (and/or demons) that control the world of matter. The practical cabala combines those natural sciences with a philological and allegorical belief in the creative power of the letter. But for Rabelais, who rejected the superstitious aspects of those sciences, their role as empirical disciplines was most important. In an investigation of the empirical sciences man establishes a dialogue with the world of nature that leads to self-understanding and points the way to knowledge of God. Empirical knowledge is limited, however, by the uncertainty of sensory perception; human wisdom ultimately depends on the philosophical dialectic of intuition for its fullest achievement.

The educational program Rabelais outlines in his literary work emphasizes quite forcibly the necessity of direct study of Nature. In his letter to Pantagruel, for example, Gargantua insists on the importance of experience through a dynamic dialogue with environment. The environment includes not only the society of Paris, but also the world of Nature in which Pantagruel participates. He is admonished in gigantic fashion to study all forms of aquatic and aerial life, to have knowledge of all plants and minerals, so that no phenomena remain unfamiliar to him (P/8). Similarly, he must achieve a thorough understanding of the microcosm by learning the medicine of the authorities and by dissecting cadavers.[30]

Gargantua's own education amplifies and complements the program in natural philosophy that Rabelais establishes for Pantagruel. The world of natural environment becomes a very meaningful part of his life, totally integrated into his daily activities. While at table, for example, he and his company investigate at first hand and through the authorities Pliny and Aristotle, among others, the properties of the food and drink served. In the morning and evening they study the configuration of the heavens. And on rainy days they visit shops of artists and artisans, but especially those of the apothecaries and alchemists.[31] Rabelais includes in their educational program field trips in order that they may study for themselves the characteristics of geological and biological phenomena (G/23-24). But the mere acquisition of knowledge of the world is insufficient, for it must become an integral part of the individual investigator, as Panurge's experience negatively demonstrates.

That Panurge has thorough knowledge of astronomy becomes evident upon a careful reading of his eulogy of debts and debtors (TL/3-4). Similarly, his confrontation with the physician Rondibilis demonstrates his familiarity with medicine (TL/31). But Panurge does not profit from his knowledge. He inverts universal order, and instead of modeling the cosmos of his own being on the macrocosm, he rather projects the disorder in his soul onto nature. He does not apply to himself whatever knowledge he has of medicine, but rather he twists the facts to suit himself. What he should do, and eventually does, is transcend the realm of natural phenomena through a logical control of data and a transformation of them through reason into a personalized experience.[32] Rabelais suggests that dialectical process, in part, in the allegory of Quinte Essence.

The disparity between the literal and figurative levels of the episode of the Quinte complicates considerably an interpretation of the passage. There can be no question that literally the language of Entelechie parodies the overly refined speech of the *précieux* and the syllogistic jargon of Aristotelian logic (CL/20). Through the vain activities of her disciples, perhaps best summarized in Socrates' continued contemplation of hopping flees, Rabelais undoubtedly satirizes the meaningless pursuits of philosophers and naturalists who seek wisdom of which they are humanly incapable (CL/22). But a careful reading of the text also points to a more serious meaning.

Her name and Rabelais's pointed reference to her Aristotelian source clearly designate Entelechie as the personification of the Perfection of Nature (CL/19). She surpasses her followers in wisdom to such an extent that she accomplishes what appear to be magical cures. But in reality she utilizes the harmonic forces of Nature (symbolized by an herbal organ) to cure the hopelessly ill (CL/20). Similarly, her devotees—the empirical astronomers, alchemists, and magi—in general, can master the laws of nature by hard study and continuous labor (CL/18, 22). For, as Entelechie states, her accomplishments and those of her men seem miraculous; but when the observer overcomes his ignorance and abstracts knowledge afforded by Nature he realizes the infinite forces at his disposal. He realizes too the disparity between himself and perfection and his inability to attain perfection.

In the separate but closely related symbols of food and the chess ballet Rabelais points out the limitedness of human knowledge. At dinner Entelechie herself eats only spiritual food, "celeste ambrosie" and "nectar divin." In contrast to her guests

and followers who feast on the best foods Nature can provide
(*CL*/23), she like the residents of Ruach (*QL*/43–44) nourishes
herself on winds, abstractions, and heavenly mana. As the Hebrew word *Ruach* (modern *Ruah*) suggests she represents the
fullest accomplishment of discursive reason. For in the Cabalistic
three-part division of soul—consisting of *Nephesh* (life spirit),
Ruah (intellectual spirit), and *Neshamah* (soul)—*Ruah* corresponds to logic and *Neshamah* to angelic reason.[33] Similarly, in
the chess ballet the victory in the third *partie* of gold over silver
symbolizes the triumph of reason over non-reason (*CL*/24–25).
But simultaneously with that victory the Queen disappears defini-
tively.[34] Allegorically her disappearance suggests that as Nature
she is indeed the Perfection of discursive reason, but as the
emanative creative agent of divine intellect she embodies and
points to a higher wisdom. Man can not follow her in her ascent
to supernal wisdom. In fact, the human mind can not achieve the
perfection of discursive reason. Man must nevertheless employ it
to the fullest of his abilities while recognizing his own limitations
and the limitations of reason.

Through his empirical investigation of natural phenomena
man can learn much that is positive about the macrocosm. But
he must transform that knowledge to self-awareness; he must
incorporate it in a dynamic dialogue with the world through
which he can attain self-understanding. Knowledge of his own
nature points to the limitations of human reason and beyond to
the necessity of reliance on intuitive reason for the fullest knowledge of himself, the world, and God. From sensory perception
man can thus move to intuition, an important aspect of the
speculative Hermetic sciences.

4. THE *HIEROS GAMOS*

Beyond each of the empirical disciplines is God. Though man
attempts to reach out beyond the creation to the Creator, he can

not; for in Rabelais's thought, finite logic can not grasp the infinite. Human reason only takes man so far in his pursuit of wisdom. Through intuitive dialectic he can move still further, but
there is a gap between the two kinds of reason. The empirical
sciences only point the way. For example, astronomy and magic
demonstrate divine order and intelligence, and alchemy suggests
to its students a spiritual rebirth in natural terms. But it is especially in the metaphysical speculations of the Cabala and the
corpus hermeticum that one finds a symbolic expression of the
union of such dialectical extremes as body and soul and the corresponding discursive and intuitive reason. Rabelais adapts from
the Hermetic literature and the Cabala the image of the sphere
and the symbolic mysteries of wine and sex to express the coincidence of opposites and the completeness of man.

The Cabalistic mysteries give both form and substance to
Panurge's quest. Wine symbolizes the voyage to self-knowledge
and the pursuit of wisdom, but marriage—the ostensible goal of
Panurge's voyage—gives his undertaking both literal and figurative content. Both wine and the holy marriage are closely related
in Cabalistic traditions. In fact they both symbolize the same
mystery of supernal wisdom and the search for completeness. In
the Cabala the theme of the Exodus with which Panurge begins
his trip ($QL/1$) signifies an historical event that each individual
repeats in his own spiritual experience.[35] It is a voyage to self-
knowledge; and it depends on mystical knowledge of God,
which is equally expressed in the Cabalistic myth of Noah.

Panurge's *epilenie* extols the virtues of Noah's wine ($CL/44$).
As the story is recounted in Old Testament and Cabalistic
sources, Noah was the only righteous man of his day and, indeed,
"the first man fit to be joined in union with the ark and enter
into it." His ark represents the Ark of the Covenant and the
microcosm. His union with it symbolizes the supernal pattern of
cosmic unity and, by consequence, individual unity of the threefold soul. Through his Covenant with God he stabilizes the
world for the first time since Adam's sin. But even his righteous-

ness is not sufficient to keep him from losing his mental balance
when he probes into Adam's sin, symbolically represented by his
replanting the vineyard and making wine. During Noah's moment of drunkenness and in his *ecstasis* before supernal wisdom,
his grandson Canaan attempts to remove the "mystical symbol
of the covenant" from him. Canaan is cursed for his action, for
he sought knowledge without righteousness.[36] Thus wine in the
Cabalistic tradition is not unlike its symbolic use in the Dionysian mysteries; similarly, mana represents supernal wisdom de-
scended from Heaven. Rabelais adapts the Hebraic symbolism of
wine and mana to point to man's union with the Divine through
contemplative wisdom.

Rabelais does not specifically mention the word "union," but
his adaptation of poetic *ecstasis* suggests it (*CL*/45–46). His constant use of *joye* and *joyeuse* implies that it is as much the attain-
ment and enjoyment of wisdom as the active search for it that
he attempts to describe. But within terms of Christian mysticism
Rabelais does not present a mystical experience; he does not describe union with God *per se*. Thus, at first one might conclude
that Rabelais intended to portray a kind of intellectual experience symbolized by the inspiration of poetic furor. This interpretation is certainly correct, but it falls short of a complete analysis
of the text. It leaves unresolved the distance between the intellectual experience itself and the *ecstasis* plainly indicated in Rabelais's description. The only kind of union mentioned, however,
is the sexual union that Panurge foresees for himself with his
future wife. But it is precisely that union that in Cabalistic terms
serves as the key to understanding the mystical experience described by Rabelais. This is not an isolated example of the adaptation of the Cabala; it is rather the final meaning Rabelais gives
to the role of woman in his work.

As one might expect, Rabelais explicitly or implicitly refers to
women in the context of the natural sexual relationship with
men. For example, Theleme, which abounds with the marriage
number "six," has marriage as a primary goal (*G*/52–57).[37] The

Sibylle de Panzoust, whom Pantagruel recommends as a possible
source of wisdom and insight, horrifies Panurge by displaying
her lower anatomy at the end of their consultation (*TL*/16–17).
Similarly, the wife of the farmer in the Papefigue episode overcomes the young devil who has arranged a scratching duel with
her husband by showing him her enormous "solution de con-
tinuité en toutes dimensions" (*QL*/45–47). Even Entelechie,
whom Rabelais depicts in the most elevated terms, is playfully
and symbolically associated with the "quinte espece de verole."
Through contracting that malady one is spiritually reborn like
the phoenix of Christian and alchemical symbolism (*CL*/21).
But especially in her association with the Cabalistic Shekinah, the
feminine principle of divinity manifest in wisdom and the tree
of creation, Entelechie points to the significance of sex.[38]

Cabalistic thought symbolically expresses the *unio mystica* in
sexual terms. There is, however, only one example of symbolical
union of man with Shekinah, namely that of Moses. In all other
instances the sexual union of man and wife concretely reflects
the spiritual union of God and Shekinah, who is symbolically
identified with the "Community of Israel." She is the Queen of
the Heavens, the Daughter as well as the Bride of God. She is
also the Mother of all and the eternal woman. She is, as the last
Sephira, the Tree of Knowledge that God separated from the
Tree of Life because of Adam's sin. Final redemption for man
and for the cosmos consists in the unified state of those two trees
symbolized by the union of Shekinah with God.[39] Thus it is
that Rabelais adapts the language of Jewish mysticism to express
the ecstasy of completion.

Panurge's poetic vision of sex with his wife concretely expresses
union on three levels (*CL*/45). It portrays the individual unity
of intellect and passions, of soul and body, and of the masculine
and feminine principles, which were once *one* prior to man's
separation into two parts after Adam's sin.[40] His vision represents the cosmic unity of the physical universe and the *anima
mundi,* additional significances of the mystic fountain. And it

suggests, above all, unity of man in God through an individually interiorized experience. Rabelais leaves no doubt about the meaning of the Dive Bouteille. His language is clear. Through the use of the Cabalistic belief in the salvation of man through woman, symbolized by sexual union, he expresses the highest truth. Knowledge of God is union in the wisdom of God. Thus the mysteries of wine and sex are identical, and the two themes with which Rabelais opens his work are joined in the symbolism of the final chapters. There is no difference between the "Beuveurs tres illustres" and the "Verolez tres precieux" (G/Prol.). Through the Cabala Rabelais gives meaning to what otherwise would remain gross humor. The erotic is as important in Rabelais's thought as drinking. Both have their concrete expression and validity. But to interpret Rabelais literally is to render invalid his symbolism. Rabelais the "bon buveur" like Rabelais the erotic are fully seen in the mysteries of wine and sex. But Rabelais's use of the Cabalistic tradition is symbolical and philosophical. Rejecting the practical cabala, he adapts the philosophical aspects of the Cabala that for him and other Renaissance humanists is an integral part of a unified tradition.[41]

Unlike Postel who projected the doctrine of the Shekinah onto his irrational cult of Mother Johana, the Bride of Christ,[42] Rabelais *philosophically* follows the symbolic *unio mystica* of the *corpus hermeticum,* Christian mysticism and Renaissance Platonic poetry. San Juan de la Cruz, for example, reflects such a symbolic tradition in the physical union of the feminine soul with the masculine Christ described in his poem "En una noche oscura." [43] Similarly, Fray Luis borrows the Cabalistic image of marriage in his Christianized interpretation of the *Cantar de los Cantares.*[44] But Rabelais's marriage is closer in tone to Leo Hebraeus' conception of sexual union as symbol of the prototype of a cosmic union of sun and moon, intellect and passion, and the ideal and imperfect natures of man and all creation. On the human scale the Androgyna symbolizes for him and for Rabelais such a perfect union.[45] Similarly the *hieros gamos,* which the

Cabala and the Hermetic writings share with the Hellenistic mysteries, points to a cosmic union accomplished in the completeness of man.[46] Thus the *hieros gamos* represents on the level of human experience the philosophical dialectic while the sphere symbolizes the cosmic coincidence of opposites in God.

Panurge's marriage is literally the means to his "salvation," for his decision to marry shows that he has restored balance in body and soul. Through marriage he maintains his reason. Allegorically, his projected union represents his empirical dialogue with nature, his philosophical discourse and his intuitive dialectic. At each of those levels he achieves self-knowledge and through self-knowledge a oneness with himself, with the empirical world of Nature, with the convivial realm of society, and with God. He can achieve his completeness only by means of the intuitive dialectic. Through his restored balance Panurge reflects the perfect harmony and order of creation, which is similarly achieved through the dialogic mean. The One makes all things harmonious, reconciles all opposites, and links all extremes. In God the world of Ideas and Nature both reflect the unity of divine essence.

The Hermetic sciences of astrology, alchemy, magic, and the Cabala serve as a primary expression of Rabelais's dialogic experience. As empirical sciences they are a means to a dynamic relationship with the world. Man may invert the knowledge he acquires from the realm of Nature into a diabolic search for power and materialistic enrichment. Or he may employ his natural discursive reason to learn about himself and his environment. Then his human reason will point toward knowledge of self and beyond to the intuitive dialectic. Man's ultimate knowledge is dependent on God; through it he attains a harmonic relationship with himself and with all creation.

NOTES

1. Walter Mönch, *Die italienische Platonrenaissance*, pp. 1–41.

2. Montaigne arrives at similar conclusions in his "Apologie de Raimond Sebond," *Essais*, II, xii, and "De l'expérience," III, xiii.

3. For example, *G*, ch. 10; *TL*, ch. 46; *CL*, ch. 42.

4. For example, *G*, chs. 1, 3, 10, 23, 39; *TL*, chs. 13, 27, 32; *QL*, chs. 8, 17, 55; *CL*, chs. 26, 30, 39.

5. The reference to the "livres de prime philosophie" appears in the part of the "Prologue" of Book V considered spurious. But similar associations lie at the heart of the episode of Quinte Essence (*CL*, chs. 18–25). For a discussion of the traditional association of Aristotle and the Hermetic sciences in the Middle Ages and Renaissance, see Lynn Thorndike, *A History of Magic and Experimental Science*, III, 96–102, 153–62, 402–23, 568–84; V, 48, and *passim*. The "prime philosophie" cited is apparently expressed in a "Tractatus Aristotelis alchymistae ad Alexandrum Magnum, de lapide philosophico" and a "Livre de Magie" of the pseudo-Aristotle. See Jehan Thenaud, *Traité de poesie*, fol. 29vo; C. G. Jung, *Psychology and Alchemy, Collected Works*, trans. R. F. C. Hull, XII, 472, 482.

6. In general, for a discussion of the relation of Platonic to Aristotelian traditions, see Philip Merlan, *From Platonism to Neoplatonism*, and *Monopsychism, Mysticism, Metaconsciousness: Problems of the Soul in the Neoaristotelian and Neoplatonic Tradition*. For the origins of the Hermetic sciences, see Festugière, *La Révélation d'Hermès*, I, 1–88. And for a discussion of the origins of the Cabala, see S. Karppe, *Etude sur les origines et la nature du 'Zóhar'*, pp. 501–81, and Henri Sérouya, *La Kabbale, ses origines, sa psychologie mystique, sa métaphysique*, pp. 31–84.

7. For example, Stanley G. Eskin, "Physis and Antiphysie: The Idea of Nature in Rabelais and Calcagnini," *Comparative Literature*, XIV (1962), 167–73.

8. Eskin, *loc. cit.*, gives an analysis of Rabelais's debt to Calcagnini.

9. Plato, *Timaeus*, 90a/d, compares man to a tree whose head is rooted in the air. See also Plutarch, *Moralia*, 400b, 600f.

10. Francesco Colonna, *Hypnerotomachia Poliphili*, fol. y-y iii^{vo}, and *Le Songe de Poliphile*, trans. Claudius Popelin, II, 246–57, and p. 246, n.1. See also the edition of Giovanni Pozzi and Lucia A. Ciapponi, I,

354, where the signatures of the original folio-edition are bracketed. Rabelais corrects the order of Colonna's listing of planets.

11. See Jean Pierre de Mesmes, *Les inſtitutions aſtronomiques,* pp. 24–27, and Auguste Bouché-Leclercq, *L'Aſtrologie grecque,* pp. 35–71.

12. *Cf.* Aristotle, *On the Heavens,* 268a–313b, *On Coming-to-be and Passing Away,* 328b–336b; Plato, *Timaeus,* 53c–61e; and Pierre Duhem, *Le Syſtème du monde,* I, 36–41.

13. For passages in Rabelais on the completeness of Nature, see *G,* chs. 5, 10; on the immortality of the species and on individual natures, *G,* chs. 9, 20; *TL,* chs. 8, 20; *QL,* ch. 27, *et pass.* On the order of Nature, see *G,* chs. 6, 23, 31; *P,* ch. 15; *TL,* chs. 31, 48; *QL,* ch. 27; *CL,* ch. 2. See also Arthur O. Lovejoy and George Boas, *Primitivism and Related Ideas in Antiquity,* Boas, *Essays on Primitivism in the Middle Ages,* and Hiram Haydn, *The Counter-Renaissance,* pp. 293–554.

14. *Pantagrueline prognoſtication,* i. ed. Plattard, V, 204–205, for an enumeration of members of the hierarchy of being.

15. As is generally known, the term "geocosm" designates the earth as a cosmos. By reconstructing the parallel descriptions to agree with the correct order of planets and appropriate gems, one can tabulate the following list:

I	Saturne	saphir	azure	plomb elutian	grüe
II	Jupiter	hiacinthe	(rouge)	estain jovetian	aigle
III	Mars	rubis ballay	pourpre	airain corinthien	lion
IV	Phoebus	diamant anachite	(foudre)	or orbrizé	coq
V	Venus	emeraude	(vert)	cuyvre	columbe
VI	Mercure	agathe	(varié)	hydrargyre	cigogne
VII	Luna	selenite	blanc	argent	lévrier

Rabelais undoubtedly based his list on a compilator such as Cornelius Agrippa, *De occulta philosophia, Opera,* I, 36–43.

16. Duhem, *Syſtème du monde,* VIII, 368–69, 421–23.

17. Festugière, *La Révélation d'Hermès,* I, 123–86, 283–308. Rabelais does not suggest anywhere that he himself prescribed the use of amulets in his own medical practice as did other humanists such as Ficino.

18. See also Rabelais, *Almanach pour l'an 1535,* ed. Plattard, V, 219, and ed. Boulenger, p. 929, where Rabelais attributes the description of man as a naturally curious creature to Aristotle.

19. The Cabala is clearly a part of the tradition of the *prisca theologia,* which was traced back to Moses and/or Adam.

20. Rabelais's reference to the "art de Lullius" may well be directed against the *ars brevis*, but it is much more likely that Rabelais had in mind the several alchemical treatises attributed to Lull. See Arthur Edward Waite, *Lives of Alchemyſtical Philosophers*, pp. 68–88. On Du Bellay, see Jean Plattard, *Vie de François Rabelais*, pp. 168–70, and on comets, see Bouché-Leclercq, *Aſtrologie*, pp. 348–69.

21. The first edition bore the title *Prognoſtication . . . pour l'an mil DXXXIII*, the second changed the date to 1535, and finally Rabelais adopted the more satirical designation *pour l'an perpetuel*. See Rabelais, ed. Plattard, V, 202, n.1, and ed. Marty-Laveaux, "Bibliographie," VI, 346–47; "Commentaires," IV, 353–54. Although I find somewhat extreme his tendency to find in Rabelais strong evidence of occultism, the chapter on alchemy and astrology in Paul Naudon, *Rabelais franc-maçon*, pp. 111–29, offers helpful insights.

22. *Pantagrueline prognoſtication*, "Au liseur," i, ed. Plattard, V, 202–205. See Charles Perrat, "Sur un tas de prognostications de Louvain," in *François Rabelais: Quatrième centenaire*, pp. 60–73.

23. *Almanach de 1533*, ed. Plattard, V, 217–18.

24. *Almanach de 1535*, ed. Plattard, V, 219–21. See Duhem, *Système du monde*, VIII, 443–501.

25. *Pantagrueline prognoſtication*, ii–x, ed. Plattard, V, 205–16, esp. 215–16.

26. See C. G. Jung, *Psychology and Alchemy, Collected Works*, trans. R. F. C. Hull, XII, 219–21.

27. The wolf was a symbol of evil in medieval times, as Lewis Spence points out in *An Encyclopaedia of Occultism*, p. 436. See also Auguste Bouché-Leclercq, *Hiſtoire de la divination dans l'antiquité*, I, 146. The sword is a necessary instrument in magical practice according to the *Liber Quartus* of the *De occulta philosophia* attributed to Agrippa. For a discussion of the fictitious dates of the *Opera omnia* in which it was published as well as the authenticity of the fourth book, see Auguste Prost, *Les sciences et les arts occultes au XVIᵉ siècle: Corneille Agrippa, sa vie et ses œuvres*, II, 517–21; Helda Bullotta Barracco, "Saggio bio-bibliografico su Enrico Cornelio Agrippa di Nettesheim," *Rassegna di filosofia*, VI, 3, 236–44; and Waite, *The Book of Ceremonial Magic*, pp. 77–79. The authenticity of the book of magic is not essential to the identity of Agrippa and Her Trippa. Its attribution to Agrippa soon after his death is an added indication of the legend of magic that grew up around him during and after his lifetime. See Prost, I, 1–13, II, 460–62.

28. Bouché-Leclercq, *Hiſtoire de la divination*, I, 176–88, 330–43.

29. See also *TL*, ch. 14, where Pantagruel appeals to "Caballistes et Massorethz" for recognition of good and bad angels and Waite, *Ceremonial Magic*, pp. 24–133; and *The Holy Kabbalah*, pp. 517–34.

30. *Cf.* Charles G. Nauert, Jr., "Agrippa in Renaissance Italy: the Esoteric Tradition," *Studies in the Renaissance*, VI (1959), 195–222.

31. In the Renaissance it was not uncommon to find an apothecary who was both herbalist and alchemist, or an alchemist who manufactured pigments, dyes, earthenware, paper, and who prepared herbs, minerals, and metals for medicinal or other practical uses. See George Sarton, *Six Wings: Men of Science in the Renaissance*, pp. 104–108.

32. *Cf.* Charles de Bouelles, *De sapiente*, xix–xxviii, pp. 340–58, and Cassirer, *Individual and the Cosmos*, pp. 88–92. For Bouelles an uninterrupted dialectical process moves from sensory perception to knowledge of God by means of self-understanding; for Rabelais discursive reason is by its very nature limited, and ultimate knowledge depends on the intuitive dialectic as it does in the thought of Cusanus.

33. *The Zohar*, trans. Harry Sperling, *et al.*, II, 205b–206a (pp. 280–81); III, 141b–142b (409–414). The second series of numbers refer to the pages of the edition cited, the first are standard references. See also Waite, *Kabbalah*, pp. 241–53.

34. As is generally known, Rabelais adapts his description of the chess ballet from Colonna, *Hypnerotomachia*, sig. G–viii, trans. Popelin, I, 191–95. See also Lazar Sainéan, "Le cinquième livre de Rabelais: son authenticité et ses parties constitutives," in *Problèmes littéraires du XVIe siècle*, pp. 254–56. For a general discussion of the ballet as a chess game, see Gaston Legrain, "Rabelais et les échecs," *RSS*, XV (1928), 151–55, who presents an analysis of Rabelais's description of moves and rules in the historic perspective of chess in the fifteenth and sixteenth centuries. For the musical aspects of the ballet, see Nan Cooke Carpenter, *Rabelais and Music*, pp. 63–68, 87–96. Boulenger, who follows the manuscript, includes this paragraph at the end of Ch. 23, pp. 835–36, *i.e.*, at the conclusion of the dinner. Inasmuch as the description of the ballet is omitted from the manuscript, the reference to the Queen's disappearance indicates both a lacuna in the manuscript reading and an inappropriate location of the paragraph in Boulenger's edition. Since the Queen appears several times in the narrative after the earlier dances, the paragraph can only apply to the chess ballet. This is apparent, moreover, from the additional details of the continuation of the voyage that are included in the passage.

35. *Cf.* Psalms 114 (113) and Gershom G. Scholem, *Major Trends in Jewish Mysticism*, pp. 19–20.

36. *Zohar*, I, 59b–73b (192–250), especially 59b (193) and 73a–73b (248–50). See also William Stirling, *The Canon: An Exposition of the Pagan Mystery Perpetuated in the Cabala as the Rule of all the Arts*, pp. 68–87.

37. *Cf.* Screech, *Rabelaisian Marriage*, pp. 29–33.

38. For a summary of the Cabalistic cosmological symbolism of the moon and its eventual union with the sun as a depiction of the union of the Shekinah with God, see *Zohar*, I, 16b–17a, 20a, 64a, 75b (70–72, 84, 209, 255). A resumé of "The Cosmic Scheme of the *Zohar*," is given in appendix, Vol. II, 397–99. See also Waite, *Kabbalah*, 161–63, 341–77.

39. The principal Cabalistic doctrines of Divine union are set forth in the *Zohar*, III, 49b–51b, 54b–55a, 57a–57b, 63b, 85a, 88b–89a, 99b, 102b, 114a, 125a–138b, 140b (152–58, 167–69, 175–79, 198, 258, 270–74, 303, 313, 340, 351–97, 405–406). For a careful study of those doctrines, see Gershom G. Scholem, *On the Kabbalah and its Symbolism*, trans. Ralph Manheim, especially pp. 104–117, 138–57, and also his *Jewish Mysticism*, pp. 225–35.

40. *Zohar*, III, 55a, 57b (168–70, 178–79). The parallelism with the Androgyna myth is obvious. The text of the *Zohar* explains the facility with which Leo Hebraeus reconciled the two accounts. See Leo Hebraeus, trans. Tyard, I, 222–53.

41. François Secret, in *Les Kabbalistes chrétiens de la Renaissance*, p. 166, concludes his discussion of Rabelais with this comment: "Et sans verser dans la chimère d'un Rabelais occultiste, on trouve surtout au *Quart livre* où se multiplient les mots hébreux, témoignage d'un certain intérêt de Rabelais pour la kabbale. . . ." Rabelais's use of Cabalistic doctrines would certainly indicate more than a passing interest in the tradition, while his philosophical adaptation of it would, as Secret indicates, preclude the "occult" significance that a modern reader might incorrectly attach to his use of the tradition.

42. Guillaume Postel, *La Vierge vénitienne*, trans. Henri Morard, especially pp. 37–38, and *Absconditorum Clavis*, trans. Bibliothèque rosicrucienne, 2 s., no. 3, pp. 36–39. See also William James Bouwsma, "*Concordia Mundi*": *The Career and Thought of Guillaume Postel (1510–1581)*, pp. 14–17, 37–46, and Secret, *Le Zôhar chez les Kabbalistes chrétiens de la Renaissance*, pp. 51–52.

43. San Juan de la Cruz, *Vida y Obras*, ed. Crisogono de Jesus, et al., pp. 507–868, 871–1121. See Helmut Hatzfeld, "Los elementos constituyentes de la poesía mística," in *Actas del primer congreso internacional de hispanistas celebrado en Oxford del 6 al 17 de septiembre de*

1962, ed. Frank Pierce and Cyril A. Jones, pp. 319–25. See also Leo Spitzer, "Three Poems on Ecstasy," in *A Method of Interpreting Literature*, pp. 21–45. The first of the three poems discussed, John Donne's "The Extasie" (published in 1633), describes the Neoplatonic union of two souls that have gone forth from their bodies and serves, therefore, as an example of the non-physical conception of human love in the purely "Platonic" tradition of the Renaissance.

44. Fray Luis de León, *Obras completas castellanas,* ed. Felix García, pp. 61–208. See also the introductory comments of García, pp. 43–60, and Secret, *Kabbalistes,* pp. 137–38.

45. Leo Hebraeus, *Dialoghi d'amore,* ed. Gebhardt, I, foll. 28–37, III, foll. 15–22, 82–94vo. See also Edward F. Meylan, "L'évolution de la notion d'amour platonique," *HR,* V (1938), 418–42, and Secret, *Kabbalistes,* pp. 79–83, 210–11, 316, for a review, respectively, of the Platonic and Cabalistic elements and influence of the *Dialoghi.*

46. Hermes Trismegistus, *Corpus Hermeticum,* II, 17; IX, 3–4, ed. A. D. Nock and A.-J. Festugière, I, 39, 97 and *Hermetica,* ed. Walter Scott, I, 144–45, 180–81. See also Festugière, *Révélation d'Hermès,* II, 548–51, and for a discussion of the *hieros gamos* in antiquity, see Richard Reitzenstein, *Die Hellenistischen Mysterienreligionen,* pp. 245–52. Similar images are found in Philo Judaeus, *De cherubim,* 40–52, ed. Jean Gorez, in *Les Œuvres,* III, 38–45.

he Rabelaisian dialectic is dynamic, and through its imitation of the divine cosmic dialogue it gives man the potential of self-deification. The sphere, which embodies the principles of immanence and transcendence, symbolizes the essential harmonic unity of the extremes in God. Similarly, the circle or sphere often serves to portray the completeness of man that for Rabelais can be attained only through the dialectic of the coincidence of opposites. But a major difference exists between the application of the images and their meaning. God transcends the world of intellect and nature, while man seeks always to attain the perfection of completeness. For God the image of the sphere is at best an approximation and, in terms of negative theology, a limitation of the divine nature; it must of necessity fall short of the mark. For man the circle is an ideal limit toward which he looks but which he can never reach. Thus on the human scale of Rabelais's literary work the Platonic-Hermetic dialectic not only demonstrates the means by which Rabelais expresses his thought but also becomes the ideal that he sets for himself and his fellow man.

The cosmic tension of the Platonic dialectic is reflected in the play on appearance and reality basic to Rabelaisian imagery and allegory. Similarly, the principle of world harmony that serves as a mean between intellect and matter in Plato's philosophy becomes Rabelais's ideal. For Rabelais the myth of the Androgyna symbolizes the adaptation of cosmic order as reason on the level of the microcosm, as *caritas* (justice) on the social level of the state, and as love in individual human relationships. *Pantagruélisme* embodies those principles of *caritas* and looks beyond to the dialogue between man and his creator. Man has his source in God, and he must return to God. The highest good man can achieve is the enjoyment of the Good. His striving for that *voluptas* is "folly." It is an individualized intuitive experience. Yet his struggle toward God through the philosophical dialectic manifests itself in convivial relationships with his fellow man.

Wine in Rabelais's literary work symbolizes most concretely the logical nature of his dialectic. At the literal level, drinking describes the conviviality necessary for dialogue. Social conversation points beyond to the exchange of ideas in the philosophical *convivium*. The willingness to talk demonstrates the desire to learn through orderly and reasonable discourse. And the knowledge attained through dialogue anticipates the wisdom of the intuitive dialectic. Intuition is the highest means of dialogue of which man is capable, and by means of the intuitive mode he establishes oneness with himself and meaningful relationships with his fellowmen and God.

The Hermetic sciences demonstrate best the unity of the Platonic-Hermetic dialectic and the completeness of man. Through the empirical investigation of the world man exercises his discursive reason, that faculty of the soul that by definition is specifically human. The logical sciences of astronomy, alchemy, magic, and the Cabala lead to an understanding of the world and of man himself. He can invert the knowledge he has acquired through an application of the black arts. Or he can transform that knowledge into a dynamic dialogue with the world that leads to self-understanding and to wisdom in God. The empirical sciences only point, however, to intuitive wisdom; for that experience depends on divine will. Rabelais adapts the *ecstasis* of the Dionysian *furor poeticus* and of the Cabalistic mysteries of wine and the *hieros gamos* to symbolize the union of man with God. Through unification with his source man achieves completeness. Through the wisdom of the intuitive dialectic he bridges the gap between soul and body just as God unifies within himself the worlds of the ideal and of matter. Thus the Platonic-Hermetic dialectic of the coincidence of opposites expresses Rabelais's conception of the dynamic unity that man can achieve within himself, with his fellowmen, with his environment, and with God. But that dialectic equally points to the human factor. Man can never achieve oneness, but for Rabelais he must actively and continually strive for that ideal.

APPENDIX

HE AUTHENTICITY OF THE *CIN-QUIESME LIVRE* AND THE THEMATIC UNITY OF RABELAIS'S FIVE BOOKS

The study of Rabelais's literary work in the perspective of the Platonic-Hermetic tradition has led to the conclusion that Rabelais shares with that tradition the dialectic of opposites. Upon superficial investigation Rabelais's work seems to be an example of philosophical eclecticism, but a careful re-evaluation of his images and allegorical myths has demonstrated a unified view of the human condition. Moreover, the dialectic in which Rabelaisian symbolism has its basis points to the thematic unity of his five books and to the authenticity of the last book. A review of the several themes of the Platonic-Hermetic tradition in their textual sequence will show that those themes are not only present throughout the five books but also that Book V serves as a logical and necessary conclusion to the first four books. Such evidence will add weight to the arguments for the authenticity of the *Cinquiesme Livre.*

The first doubts about the authenticity of Book V seem to have appeared early in the seventeenth century. In his discussion of the problem, Marty-Laveaux cites the *Prosopographie* of Antoine du Verdier, which attributes the *Isle sonante* to "un Escholier de Valence," and the *Diverses leçons* of Louis Guyon, who denies Rabelais's authorship of the last book on the basis of its anti-Catholic sentiment. Guyon adds somewhat vaguely that he was at Paris when the book was written and knows well "qui en fut l'autheur, qui n'estoit Medecin." In spite of these objections Rabelais's readers of the seventeenth and eighteenth centuries did not question the authenticity of Book V. Le Duchat, for example, in editing Rabelais's works (1711) stated affirmatively that the fifth book was Rabelais's and that it demonstrated both his style and spirit. He refuted the validity of the quasi-contemporary objections, for he saw in Verdier's comment a confusion of the *Isle sonante* with the apocryphal *Fanfreluche & Gaudichon* and in Guyon's statement an attempt to defend uncritically the orthodoxy and medical reputation of Rabelais.

It was not until the middle of the nineteenth century, when the manuscript was rediscovered, that an attempt was made to prove the last book inauthentic. Marty-Laveaux, considering the factual and stylistic objections, concludes, nevertheless, that Rabelais had probably left fragments, perhaps intended originally for earlier books, and rough drafts that were assembled by an imitator.[1] Toward the turn of the century Arthur Tilley reviewed the objections to the authenticity of the book, concurred with Le Duchat in rejecting the comments of Verdier and Guyon, and accepted without question the genuineness of the last sixteen chapters (the episodes of Lanternois and the Dive Bouteille) and with less certainty the fourth chapter.[2] Since that time, with the exception of a very limited study by Birch-Hirschfeld, critical analyses have tended to accept the authenticity of the entire book with minor qualifications.[3]

In 1905 Lefranc and Boulenger edited *L'Isle sonante.* Having compared the text of 1562 with the first complete edition of 1564 and with the manuscript they concluded that Rabelais's editors had probably used the plan, notes, and rough drafts that he left to publish the complete work.[4] This conclusion, now generally accepted, has left open the possibility of interpolations but leaves no doubt that the fifth book in its entirety was planned and written at least in first draft by Rabelais.[5] The most complete analysis of the fifth book based on language, style, and sources has been made by Sainéan who concludes from these criteria that the work is authentic, with the exception of four short interpolations. Sainéan reached his decision only after a complete analysis of the major episodes and a careful comparison of linguistic habits in Rabelais's five books.[6] More recently Car-

penter has added further evidence for Rabelais's authorship in
her comparative study of musical terminology throughout the
five books.[7] To these studies can be added the additional criteria
suggested by the analysis of the Platonic and Hermetic tradition;
for each of the themes points to the continuity of composition.

Rabelais states his interest in Platonism in humanistic terms
in the letter to Pantagruel (*P*/8). It appears as the basis for his
symbolism throughout the five books. The images of the *silenes*
and *sustantificque mouelle* (G/Prol.) show that the Platonic
play on appearance and reality gives Rabelais's symbolism and
allegory their fullest meaning. The Androgyna and color
symbolism of Gargantua's livery (*G*/9–10) suggest his Augustinian adaptation of the Platonic harmony-order as *caritas*. In the
first chapter of the *Tiers Livre* Rabelais suggests *caritas* as the
principle of conduct for his philosopher-kings of the first two
books. Then, through Panurge's eulogy of debts (*TL*/3–4), he
states the theme of Platonic love as universal harmony. It is this
theme, expressed as temperance on the level of human experience, that underlies Panurge's quest, first in the divinatory
consultations (*TL*/10–28), then in the *convivium* (*TL*/29–36),
and finally in the voyage that culminates in the visit to the Dive
Bouteille (*CL*/34–47). The allegorical quest points, moreover, to
Rabelais's conception of knowledge, expressed in the dualistic
symbols of wine and food.

Wine, in itself, is reminiscent of Rabelais's positive acceptance
of the physical realm as good within itself. Associated with social
conviviality, seen in the dinner of tripes (*G*/4–5) and the symposium (*TL*/29–36), wine corresponds to discursive reason and
human knowledge acquired empirically. The symbolic value of
wine, suggested in the "Prologue" to Gargantua and expressed
again through the consultations of the *Tiers Livre,* corresponds

to the philosophical dialectic. The symbolism of wine is closely associated with the voyage theme. The image of the *pantagruelion* presented at the end of the *Tiers Livre* (*TL*/49–52), a reminder of Rabelais's ideal *pantagruélisme* (QL/Prol.), and the emblematic drinking vessels that serve as ensigns for the fleet (QL/1) anticipate the imagery of the Dive Bouteille.

Throughout the voyage itself there are constant reappearances of Platonic symbols. The pictorial representation of the *Idées* on the Isle de Medamothi (*QL*/2) and the *parolles gelées* (*QL*/55–56) of the *Quart Livre* are similar to the *febves en gosses* of the "Prologue" to the last book. This image, which appears in the part of the "Prologue" considered apocryphal, restates the theme of three-fold interpretation. The editor of this passage, assuming that it is an interpolation, shows particularly keen insight into Rabelais's thought. To the image of the *febves* he adds an allusion to Marguerite de Navarre, another historical indication of Rabelais's Platonism, and a lengthy discussion on wine, replete with references to *nectar divin* and the *fons Cabalin*. These several elements, considered together, would seem to indicate that this passage is essentially Rabelaisian and probably authentic. The images are not only in keeping with those of the first four books, but they anticipate the symbolism of the last episodes.[8]

The polar relation of human knowledge and philosophical vision is presented in the episodes of the Pays de Satin (*CL*/30–31) and of the related Lanternois and Dive Bouteille. Natural science, represented by the Lantern-bearing Aristotle (*CL*/30), serves as a guide and complement to the metaphysics of Plato, portrayed by the Lanterne who was the friend of the Platonist Lamy (*CL*/32–33[2]). Although Platonism defines the philosophical dialectic, Plato like the Lanterne can only lead the individual to the realm of intellect. The vision of the Ideas must be acquired through self-knowledge, a dialectical process symbolized by the Dionysian mosaics of the Temple (*CL*/38–40) and the architectural fountain (*CL*/42). In Panurge's triumph Rabelais shows the full significance of the truth of wine in its relation to Socratic

self-knowledge. He thus concludes the fifth book with themes
with which he begins the first. The last three episodes are the
appropriate conclusion to the philosophical themes and symbolism
of the first four books. The seeming polarity of human and
divine knowledge is resolved in the poetizing in the final episode.
Just as Rabelais emphasizes both the contemplative and active
aspects of human intellect, through the symbolism of wine he
points to both empirical and intuitive knowledge in the Hermetic
sciences.

Rabelais's criticism of the abuses of astrology and alchemy is
first set forth in the letter to Pantagruel (P/8), while his acceptance of both as natural sciences is seen in Gargantua's educational program (G/23–24). In the Picrocholine war, Rabelais
satirizes the superstitious acceptance of astrology, demonical
magic, and the Cabala (G/35–36). Similarly in *Pantagruel* he
attacks, through the language of alchemy, the vanities of the
alchemists and the sale of indulgences (P/17). In the *Tiers Livre*
he uses Her Trippa as the representative of both judicial astrology
and black magic, leaving no doubt about his condemnation of
both (TL/25). The episodes of the Papimanes in the *Quart
Livre* (48–54) and the Chats fourrez and Apedeftes in the
Cinquiesme Livre (11–16) show the same metaphorical use of
alchemical language in satire of ecclesiastic or judicial materialism
and, indirectly, the abuses of the Hermetic sciences.[9] But just as
Rabelais's criticism of the vanities of these sciences is a constant
motif throughout the five books, so his acceptance of them is
equally prevalent.

In his general treatment of divination in the *Tiers Livre,*
Rabelais manifests his belief in the philosophical vision attained,
for example, through dreams (TL/14) and the poet's swan
song (TL/21). And in the *Quart Livre* he suggests in the discussion of the death of Heroes and Daimons his belief in the
efficacy of meteors and comets as presages (QL/26–27). The two
aspects of divination are textually related through the description
of the death of Du Bellay, philosophically through the idea of

Providence. In the *Cinquiesme Livre* Rabelais gives astrology a symbolic meaning through the iconology of the fountain. Similarly, the visit to the realm of Quinte Essence (*CL*/19–25) suggests, as does the color symbolism of the episode of the Chats fourrez (*CL*/14), a philosophical use of alchemy. The initiatory rituals of the Dive Bouteille point to the symbolic use of magic, and both these episodes indicate Rabelais's use of Jewish mysticism.

In the first two books Rabelais satirizes the superstitious abuses of the Cabala in the Picrocholine war. The *Tiers Livre* shows similar treatment in the satire of the *caballe monastique* (*TL*/15) and the demonology of Her Trippa (*TL*/25). But in several references in the first three books Rabelais anticipates the importance of the Cabala in the last two books.[10] Although the *Quart Livre* and *Cinquiesme Livre* both show Rabelais's increased use of Hebrew terms, the mysteries of wine and sex inspired by Jewish mysticism are also present in the earlier books. The position of woman as arbiter of taste in Theleme (*G*/55–57) anticipates Rabelais's acceptance of woman as the means of salvation of man and the cosmos. His gradual development of the theme is seen in the consultation with the Sibylle (*TL*/16–18), in the tale of the Papefiguiere (*QL*/46), and in Entelechie (*CL*/19–25). The mystery of sex reaches its fullest meaning in the "mysticism" of the Dive Bouteille (*CL*/42–47). There, in combination with the symbolism of wine, suggested by Noah, Rabelais's adaptation of Shekinah as the manifestation of Wisdom and as the embodiment of Womanhood serves as the means to understanding his mysticism and the relation of the two mysteries symbolized by the *Beuveurs* and *Verolez* of the "Prologue" to *Gargantua*. The last episode also shows the relationship of the Cabala to Hermetism, for in enumerating the *prisci theologi* and repeating the Hermetic metaphor of the sphere, Rabelais points to the unity of Platonism and Hermetism throughout the work. Thus, it is clear that there is a continuity in Rabelais's use of the Hermetic tradition throughout the five books.

The continuity of Rabelais's religious beliefs also points to the authenticity of the last book. The first eight chapters of Book V satirize in the *Isle sonante* the whole ecclesiastical structure. Through an attack on fasting and the regimentation of ecclesiastical life by the canonical hours, Rabelais again shows that excesses make men less than human; in this instance he humorously depicts the clergy as birds. He also includes in his satire a direct reference to the gluttony and sexual promiscuity of these useless creatures, who spend their time eating and singing, never working (*CL*/1–8). These are the motifs that appear throughout Rabelais's religious criticism and suggest the authenticity of this episode as well as that of the Isle des Esclots (*CL*/27-28) in which Rabelais attacks through the Frères Fredons monastic materialism and Lent. On the positive side of religious belief, the episode of the Dive Bouteille shows the relationship of the individual to God, and gives the fullest expression of Rabelais's philosophical "Mysticism." The image of the sphere and the reference to the *Dieu caché* (*CL*/47) suggest the immanence and transcendence of theology and the coincidence of extremes of philosophical dialectic. Thus the last book not only points to the continuity of religious beliefs, but also through the resolution of theological and philosophical opposites to the unity of Rabelais's thought in his five books.

A review of the episodes of the *Cinquiesme Livre* would show that one or more aspects of the Platonic and Hermetic tradition is basic to each in succession. The "Prologue" contains Platonic images, historical allusions, and wine symbolism. The *Isle sonante* (1–8) is an example of Rabelais's use of Platonic harmony in satire of religious extremes. The Platonic image of the celestial tree is basic to Rabelais's satire in the Isle des Ferremens (9), while he combines the Ideas with demonology in the satire of the court in the Isle de Cassade (10). Alchemy is the motif common to the episodes of the Chats fourrez (11–14) and the Apedeftes (16). Platonic harmony underlies Rabelais's satire of the Outrés (17) and, combined with alchemy, magic, and the Cabala, the symbolism of Quinte Essence (18–25). In the Isle des Odes (26) and the Isle des Esclots (27–29) Rabelais criticizes human depravity through the use of the motifs of the Ideas and harmony. The synthesis of Aristotelian and Platonic philosophies and the dialogue between empirical and intuitive knowledge are suggested by Ouy-dire (30–31) and Lanternois (32–33[2]).

Every theme of the Platonic and Hermetic tradition discussed appears in the episode of the Dive Bouteille. Rabelais's symbolism of wine is represented in the architectural decorations and motto of the Temple. The fountain and stairway suggest the symbolic use of astrology to depict the harmony of the spheres. The initiatory rites combine the Dionysian mysteries with Apollonian poetic furor, magic, and the Cabalistic mysteries of wine and sex; they all lead to self-knowledge and knowledge of God. The seemingly contradictory Aristotelian natural science and Platonic philosophical dialectic are resolved in the infinity of the Hermetic sphere. More than any other episode the Dive Bouteille points to the unity of Rabelais's dialectic, a unity consistent with the continuity of theme and composition throughout the five books. The Platonic and Hermetic tradition expresses that unity and points to the authenticity of the *Cinquiesme Livre.*

APPENDIX: NOTES

1. Marty-Laveaux, "Commentaire," in Rabelais, *Œuvres*, IV, 309–14.

2. Arthur Tilley, "The Authenticity of the Fifth Book of Rabelais," *Modern Quarterly of Language and Literature*, I (1898–99), 113–16.

3. Adolf Birch-Hirschfeld, *Das fünfte Buch des Pantagruel und sein Verhältnis zu den authentischen Büchern des Romans*, pp. 1–35.

4. Jacques Boulenger, "Introduction," in Rabelais, *L'Isle sonante*, ed. Lefranc and Boulenger, pp. i–xx. None of the critics opposed to the authenticity of Book V has set forth either careful or scholarly arguments to support its inauthenticity. They have generally chosen to ignore the favorable evidence.

5. The most recent editors have accepted this conclusion without question. See, for example, Lefranc, "Introduction," *Pantagruel*, III, xi; Boulenger, "Introduction," *Œuvres complètes*, p. 19; Plattard, "Review of L. Sainéan, *Problèmes littéraires du XVIe siècle*," *RSS*, XIV (1927), 404–405; Gaston Legrain, "Review of Jean Plattard, *Vie de François Rabelais*," *RSS*, XVI (1929), 166. The problem has been reviewed most recently by Pierre Jourda in his edition of the *Œuvres complètes*, II, 263–272; Jourda concludes that it would be impossible to resolve the problem of authenticity without the discovery of an *autographe*, but he includes the book in the corpus of Rabelais literature.

6. Sainéan, "Le *Cinquième Livre*," pp. 1–98, 251–60. The results of his detailed comparative linguistic study are found in Sainéan, *La Langue de Rabelais*, which refers to his earlier studies as well.

7. Carpenter, *Rabelais and Music*, pp. 18–29, 97–119.

8. *Cinquiesme Livre*, "Prologue," ed. Plattard, V, 1–9; the shorter manuscript reading is given by Boulenger, pp. 771–72. The problems of authenticity, together with his own objections to the authenticity of the passage, are discussed by Sainéan, "Le *Cinquième Livre*," pp. 12–14. Rabelais also refers to Marguerite in *TL*/Prol.

9. The episode of the Apedeftes has not been discussed in the course of this study. The Apedeftes, like the Chats fourrez, are personifications of judicial injustice that Rabelais once more satirizes through the language of alchemy. The episode appears as Chapter XVI in the modern editions, ed. Plattard, V, 53–59, and ed. Boulenger, pp. 811–14, while

Jean Martin includes it as Chapter VII, t. II, 25–32. The doubts about its authenticity are refuted by Boulenger, "Introduction," *L'Isle sonante*, p. xx. Rabelais's use of alchemy shows the relation of the chapter to the preceding episode and also points to its authenticity.

10. For example, *P*, Prol. and Chs. 8, 20; *TL*, Chs. 3, 14.

A. PRIMARY SOURCES

1. Rabelais

L'Abbaye de Thélème (*Gargantua, Chap. LII–LVIII*), ed. Raoul Morçay. Paris, Droz, 1934.

All the Extant Works, trans. Samuel Putnam. New York, Covici-Friede, 1929. 3 vols.

Faux autographe. B.N., Ms. fr., n.a. 709, foll. 141^r–158^v.

L'Isle sonante, ed. Abel Lefranc and Jacques Boulenger. Paris, Champion, 1905.

Lettres écrites d'Italie par François Rabelais: Décembre 1535–Février 1536, ed. V. L. Bourrilly. Paris, Champion, 1910.

Œuvres, ed. Abel Lefranc, *et al.* Paris-Genève, Champion-Droz, 1913–55. 6 tomes to date.

Les Œuvres. Lyon, Jean Martin, 1565.

Les Œuvres, ed. Charles Marty-Laveaux. Paris, Alphonse Lemerre, 1870–1902. 6 vols.

Œuvres complètes, ed. Jacques Boulenger. *Bibliothèque de la Pléiade,* XV. Paris, Gallimard, 1955.

Œuvres complètes, ed. Pierre Jourda. Paris, Garnier, 1962. 2 vols.

Œuvres complètes, ed. Jean Plattard. Paris, Société d'édition "Les Belles Lettres," 1946–48. 5 vols.

Pantagruel, ed. P. Babeau, Jacques Boulenger, and H. Patry. Paris, Champion, 1904.

Pantagruel, ed. Robert Marichal. Lyon, Association générale de l'internat et du conseil d'administration des hospices civils, 1935.

Pantagruel, ed. Verdun L. Saulnier. Paris, Droz, 1946.

Pantagruel, livre 5. B.N., Ms. fr. 2156.

Le Quart Livre, ed. Robert Marichal. Lille-Genève, Droz, 1947.

Le Tiers Livre, ed. Pierre Grimal. Bibliothèque de Cluny. Paris, Colin, 1962.

2. Other

ABAN, PIERRE D'. *Les Œuvres magiques de Henri-Corneille Agrippa.* Liège, 1788. (B.N., R.25998)

AGRIPPA VON NETTESHEIM, HEINRICH CORNELIUS. *Declamation sur l'incertitude, vanité et abus des sciences,* trans. Louis de Mayerne-Turquet. Paris, J. Durand, 1582. (B.N., Z.19077)

———. *Opera.* Lugduni, per Beringos fratres, 1510 [?].

———. *Traité de l'excellence de la femme,* trans. Lois Vivant. Paris, J. Poupy, 1578. (B.N., R.24169)

AQUINAS, THOMAS. *Summa Theologia,* trans. Fathers of the English Dominican Province. Great Books of the Western World, XIX–XX. Chicago-London-Toronto, Benton, 1952. 2 vols.

ARISTOTLE. *The Metaphysics.* trans. Hugh Tredennick. The Loeb Classical Library. London-New York, 1933–47. 2 vols.

———. *On Coming-to-Be and Passing Away,* trans. E. S. Forster. The Loeb Classical Library. London-Cambridge, 1955.

———. *On the Heavens,* trans. W. K. C. Guthrie. The Loeb Classical Library. London-Cambridge, 1939.

———. *On the Soul,* trans. W. S. Hett. The Loeb Classical Library. London-Cambridge, 1935.

———. *Parts of Animals,* trans. A. L. Peck. The Loeb Classical Library. London-Cambridge, 1937.

———. *The Physics,* trans. Philip H. Wicksteed and Francis M. Cornford. The Loeb Classical Library. London-Cambridge, 1929–34. 2 vols.

BAÏF, JEAN-ANTOINE DE. *Œuvres en rime,* ed. Charles Marty-Laveaux. Paris, Lemerre, 1881–90. 5 vols.

BOETHIUS. *The Consolation of Philosophy,* trans. W. V. Cooper. New York, Random House, 1960.

BOUELLES, CHARLES DE. *De sapiente (1509),* in Ernst Cassirer, *Individuum und Kosmos in der Philosophie der Renaissance.* Darmstadt, Wissenschaftliche Buchgesellschaft, 1963, pp. 299–412.

CASTIGLIONE, BALDESSAR. *Book of the Courtier,* trans. Charles S. Singleton. Garden City, New York, Doubleday, 1959.

CHAMPIER, SYMPHORIEN. *La nef des dames vertueuses.* Lyon, Arnollet, 1503.

CICERO, MARCUS TULLIUS. *De Divinatione* in *De Senectute, De Amicitia, De Divinatione,* trans. William Armstead Falconer. The Loeb Classical Library. London-Cambridge, 1938, pp. 214–539.

COLONNA, FRANCESCO. *Hypnerotomachia Poliphili.* Venice, Aldus Manutius, 1499.

——. *Hypnerotomachia Poliphili,* ed. Giovanni Pozzi and Lucia A. Ciapponi. Padua, Editrice Antenore, 1964. 2 vols.

——. *Le Songe de Poliphile,* trans. Claudius Popelin. Paris, Liseux, 1883. 2 vols.

Cusanus, Nicolaus. *De la docte ignorance,* trans. L. Moulinier. Paris, Alcan, 1930.

——. *Of learned ignorance,* trans. Germain Heron. New Haven, Yale University Press, 1954.

——. *Opera (Parisiis, 1514).* Frankfurt/Main, Minerva, 1962. 3 vols.

Dante Alighieri. *The Divine Comedy,* trans. John D. Sinclair. New York, Oxford, 1961. 3 vols.

Dionysius Areopagita. *Œuvres complètes,* trans. Maurice de Gandillac. Paris, Aubier, 1943.

——. *The Works,* trans. John Parker. London, James Parker, 1897. 2 vols.

Du Moulin, Antoine, trans. *La Vertu et propriété de la quinte essence de toutes choses . . . , faicte en Latin per Joannes de Rupescissa.* Lyon, Jean de Tournes, 1581. (B.N., V.21874)

Eckhart. *Meister Eckhart, a Modern Translation,* trans. Raymond Bernard Blakney. New York-London, Harper, 1941.

Erasmus, Desiderius. *Chiliadis tertiae, Centuria III. Opera omnia.* Lugduni Batavorum, Peter Vander Aa, 1703. Vol. II.

——. *The Colloquies . . . ,* ed. E. Johnson. London, Gibbings, 1900. 3 vols.

——. *The Education of a Christian Prince,* trans. Lester K. Born. New York, Columbia University Press, 1936.

——. *Moriae encomium.* Coloniae, Apud Iohan., 1534.

Euripides. *Bacchanals,* trans. Arthur S. Way. The Loeb Classical Library. London-New York, 1912. Vol. III.

Ficino, Marsilio. *Commentaire sur le Banquet de Platon,* ed.-trans. Raymond Marcel. Paris, Société d'édition "Les Belles Lettres," 1956.

——. *De la Religion chrestienne . . . ,* trans. Lefevre de la Boderie. Paris, G. Beis, 1578. (B.N., D.75661)

——. *Opera omnia,* ed. M. Sancipriano and Paul Oskar Kristeller. Torino, Bottega d'Erasmo, 1959. 2 vols.

——. *Les Trois livres de la vie . . . ,* trans. Guy Le Fèvre de La Boderie. Paris, L'Angelier, 1581. (B.N., Tc. ¹¹16)

FINÉ, ORONCE. *Les canons et documens tres amples, touchant l'usage et pratique des communs Almanachz que l'on nomme Ephemerides . . .* Paris, Regnaud Chaudière, 1551. (B.N., V.29284)

——. *La sphere du monde proprement ditte cosmographie . . .* Paris, Michel de Vascosan, 1551. (B.N., V.7643)

FONTAINE, JACQUES. *Discours de la puissance du ciel sur les corps inferieurs, et principalement de l'influence contre les astrologues judiciaires, avec une dispute des éléments contre les paracelsistes . . .* Paris, G. Gorbin, 1581. (B.N., V.21794)

——. *Discours des marques des sorciers et de la réelle possession que le diable prend sur le corps des hommes . . .* Paris, Denis Langlois, 1611. (B.N., Ln²⁷ 8344)

GALEN. *Galen on Medical Experience: First Edition of the Arabic Version with English Translation and Notes . . .* London-New York-Toronto, Oxford, 1946.

The Greek Anthology, trans. W. R. Paton. The Loeb Classical Library. London-New York, 1916–18. 5 vols.

HERMES TRISMEGISTUS. *Corpus hermeticum,* ed. A. D. Nock and A.-J. Festugière. Paris, Société d'édition "Les Belles Lettres," 1945–54. 4 vols.

——. *Hermetica, the Ancient Greek and Latin Writings which contain Religious or Philosophic Teachings ascribed to Hermes Trismegistus,* ed. Walter Scott. Oxford, Clarendon, 1924–36. 4 vols.

HÉROËT, ANTOINE. *Œuvres poétiques,* ed. Ferdinand Gohin. STFM, Paris, Droz, 1943.

Journal d'un Bourgeois de Paris sous le règne de François Premier (1515–1536), ed. Ludovic Lalanne. Société de l'Histoire de France, LXXV. Paris, Renouard, 1854.

JUAN DE LA CRUZ, SAN. *Vida y Obras,* ed. Crisogono de Jesus, *et al.* Madrid, Biblioteca de autores cristianos, 1955.

LANDINO, CHRISTOPHORO. *Libri Quattuor.* Argentoraci, Mathias Schürerius, 1508.

LA RAMÉE, PIERRE DE. *Dialectique (1555),* ed. Michel Dassonville. *Travaux d'humanisme et renaissance,* LXVII. Genève, Droz, 1964.

LE CARON, LOUIS. *Les Dialogues.* Paris, J. Longis, 1556.

LEMAIRE DE BELGES, JEAN. *Les Illustrations de Gaule et singularitez de Troye . . . ,* ed. Antoine du Moulin. Lyon, Jean de Tournes, 1549.

LEO HEBRAEUS. *De l'amour,* trans. Pontus de Tyard. Lyon, Jean de Tournes, 1551. 2 vols.

LEO HEBRAEUS. *Dialoghi d'amore,* ed. Carl Gebhardt. Heidelberg-London-Paris, Winter, 1929.

LEÓN, FRAY LUIS DE. *Obras completas castellanas,* ed. Felix García. Madrid, Biblioteca de autores cristianos, 1959.

LUCIAN. "Dionysus, An Introduction," trans. M. Harmon. The Loeb Classical Library. London-New York, 1913. Vol. I, 47–59.

———. "Praefatio, seu Bacchus," *Opera.* Amsterdam, 1843. Vol. III, 74–85.

LULL, RAMÓN. *Opera ars universalis.* Argentorati, L. Zetzneri, 1617.

———. *Opera latina.* Majorca, Ediciones españolas de Filosofía, 1961.

MARGUERITE D'ANGOULÊME. *Lettres de Marguerite d'Angoulême soeur de François Ier, reine de Navarre, publiées d'après les manuscrits de la Bibliothèque du roi,* ed. F. Génin. Paris, Renouard, 1841.

———. *Le Navire, ou Consolation du Roi François Ier à sa Soeur,* ed. Robert Marichal. Paris, Champion, 1956.

———. *Nouvelles lettres de la Reine de Navarre adressées au roi François Ier son frère,* ed. F. Génin. Paris, Renouard, 1842.

MAROT, CLÉMENT. *Les Œuvres de Clément Marot de Cahors en Quercy,* ed. Georges Guiffrey, *et al.* Paris, Schemit, *et al.,* 1875–1931. 5 vols.

MESMES, JEAN PIERRE DE. *Les institutions astronomiques contenans les principaux fondemens et premieres causes des cours et mouvemens celestes.* Paris, Michel de Vascosan, 1557. (B.N., V.1708)

MORE, THOMAS. *Opera omnia Latina, Francofurti et Lipsiae, 1689.* Frankfurt-am-Main, Minerva, 1963.

———. *De optimo respublicae statu deque nova insula Utopia, libellus vere aureus.* Basle, Jean Froben, 1518.

NUISEMENT, CLOVIS HESTEAU, SIEUR DE. *Sal, lumen & spiritus mundi philosophici: or, The Dawning of the day . . . ,* trans. R[obert] T[urner]. London, 1657.

OVID. *Metamorphoses,* trans. Frank Justus Miller. The Loeb Classical Library. London-New York, 1916. 2 vols.

PARACELSUS. *Four Treatises of Theophrastus von Hohenheim, called Paracelsus,* trans. C. Lilian Tenskin, *et al.* Baltimore, Johns Hopkins University Press, 1941.

———. *The Hermetic and Alchemical Writings,* ed. Arthur Edward Waite. London, Ellicott, 1894. 2 vols.

———. *Œuvres complètes,* trans. Grillot de Givry. Paris, Chacornac, 1913. 2 vols.

PASCAL, BLAISE. *Pensées,* ed. Leon Brunschvicg. Paris, Hachette, 1966.

PHILO JUDAEUS. *About the Contemplative Life; or, The Fourth Book of the Treatise concerning Virtues,* ed. Fred C. Conybeare. Oxford, Clarendon, 1895.

————. *De cherubim,* ed. Jean Gorez in *Les Œuvres.* Paris, Editions du Cerf, 1963. Vol. III.

PICO DELLA MIRANDOLA, GIOVANNI. *Opera,* ed. Jacob Wimpheling [Strassburg], 1504.

————. *De hominis dignitate, Heptaplus, De ente et uno, e scritti vari,* a cura di Eugenio Garin. Firenze, Vallechi, 1942.

————. *Of Being and Unity (De ente et uno),* trans. Victor Michael Hamm. Milwaukee, Wisconsin, Marquette University Press, 1943.

————. *A Platonick Discourse upon Love,* trans. Edmund G. Gardner. Boston, Merrymount, 1914.

PLATO. *Cratylus,* trans. H. N. Fowler. The Loeb Classical Library. London-New York, 1926. Vol. VI, 1–191.

————. *Laws,* trans. R. G. Bury. The Loeb Classical Library. London-New York, 1926. Vols. IX and X.

————. *Œuvres complètes.* Association Guillaume Budé. Paris, Société d'édition "Les Belles Lettres," 1951– . 13 vols.

————. *Phaedrus,* trans. H. N. Fowler. The Loeb Classical Library. London-New York, 1914.

————. *Politicus,* trans. H. N. Fowler. The Loeb Classical Library. London-New York, 1925. Vol. III, 1–195.

————. *The Republic,* trans. Paul Shorey. The Loeb Classical Library. London-New York, 1930. 2 vols.

————. *The Symposium,* trans. W. R. M. Lamb. The Loeb Classical Library. London-New York, 1925. Vol. V, 73–245.

————. *Timaeus,* trans. R. G. Bury. The Loeb Classical Library. London-New York, 1929. Vol. VII, 1–253.

PLOTINUS. *Ennéades,* ed. Emile Bréhier. Paris, Société d'édition "Les Belles Lettres," 1924–54. 6 vols.

PLUTARCHUS. *Moralia,* trans. Frank Cole Babbitt. The Loeb Classical Library. London-Cambridge, 1956– . 15 vols.

POLIZIANO, ANGELO. *Omnia Opera.* Paris, Badius, 1519.

POSTEL, GUILLAUME. *Absconditorum Clavis,* trans. Bibliothèque rosicrucienne, 2.s., no. 3. Paris, Chacornac, 1899.

POSTEL, GUILLAUME. *La Vierge vénitienne*, trans. Henri Morard. Les Classiques de l'Occulte. Paris, Chacornac, 1928.

REUCHLIN, JOHANNES. *De verbo mirifico. 1494 [and] De arte cabalistica. 1517, Faksimile-Neudruck in einem Band.* Stuttgart-Bad Cannstatt, Frommann, 1964.

RONSARD, PIERRE DE. *Hymne des daimons,* ed. A.-M. Schmidt. Paris, Michel, 1939.

――――. *Œuvres complètes,* ed. Paul Laumonier. Paris, Hachette-Droz, 1914–52. 16 vols.

SCÈVE, MAURICE. *Délie, object de plus haulte vertu,* ed. Eugène Parturier. Paris, Didier, 1961.

――――. *Œuvres poétiques complètes . . . ,* ed. Bertrand Guégan. Paris, Garnier, 1927.

TERESA, SANTA. *The Life of Saint Teresa,* trans. J. M. Cohen. Baltimore, Penguin, 1957.

THENAUD, JEHAN. *La Lignée de Saturne.* B.N., Ms. fr. 1358.

――――. *La saincte et trescrestienne cabale metrifiée.* B.N., Ms. fr. 882.

――――. *Traité de la cabale avec une lettre à François Ier.* Bibliothèque de l'Arsenal, Ms. 5061.

――――. *Traité de poesie.* B.N., Ms. fr. 2081.

THEOCRITUS. *Bucoliques grecs,* ed. Ph. E. Legrand. Paris, Société d'édition "Les Belles Lettres," 1953–60. 2 vols.

――――. Ειδυλλια *Eidyllia, hoc est parva Poëmata, XXXVI,* reddita per H. Eobanum Hessum . . . & Joachimi Comerarii. Francforti, Petri Brubachii, 1553.

THOMAS À KEMPIS. *De Imitatione Christi, Libri Quattuor.* London, Macmillan, 1867.

TYARD, PONTUS DE. *Les Discours philosophiques . . .* Paris, L'Angelier, 1587.

――――. *Mantice ou discours de la vérité de divination par astrologie.* Lyons, Jean de Tournes, 1558.

――――. *Les Œuvres poétiques,* ed. Charles Marty-Laveaux. Paris, Lemerre, 1875.

――――. *Le Solitaire premier,* ed. Silvio F. Baridon. Genève, Droz, 1950.

VILLON, FRANÇOIS. *Œuvres,* ed. Louis Thuasne. Paris, Picard, 1923. 3 vols.

The Zohar, trans. Harry Sperling, *et al.* London, Soncino, 1949. 5 vols.

B. SECONDARY SOURCES

ADHÉMAR, JEAN. "Ronsard et l'école de Fontainebleau," *BHR*, XX (1958), 344–48.

ALLEN, DON CAMERON. *The Legend of Noah: Renaissance Rationalism in Art, Science, and Letters*. Illinois Studies in Language & Literature, 33, No. 3–4. Urbana, 1949.

————. "The Rehabilitation of Epicurus and His Theory of Pleasure in the early Renaissance," *Studies in Philology*, XLI (1944), 1–15.

————. *The Star-Crossed Renaissance: the Quarrel about Astrology and its Influence in England*. Durham, N.C., Duke University Press, 1941.

ALLEN, PERCY STAFFORD. *The Age of Erasmus*. Oxford, Clarendon, 1914.

AMBELAIN, ROBERT. *La Kabbale pratique*. Paris, Niclaus, 1951.

ANAGNINE, EUGENIO. *G. Pico della Mirandola: Sincretismo religioso-filosofico. Biblioteca di cultura moderna*, CCCIV. Bari, Laterza, 1937.

ANCONA, PAOLO D'. *The Farnesina Frescoes at Rome*. Milan, Edizioni del Milione, 1956.

ARNOUX, GEORGES. *Musique platonicienne: âme du monde*. Paris, Dervy, 1960.

ASSOCIATION GUILLAUME BUDÉ, Paris. *Congrès de Tours et Poitiers*. . . . Paris, Société d'édition "Les Belles Lettres," 1954.

AUERBACH, ERICH. "Figura," *Scenes from the Drama of European Literature*. New York, Meridian, 1959.

BARAT, J. "L'Influence de Tiraqueau sur Rabelais," *RER*, III (1905), 138–55, 253–75.

BARIDON, SILVIO F. *Inventaire de la bibliothèque de Pontus de Tyard*. Genève, Droz, 1950.

BARON, HANS. "Franciscan Poverty and Civic Wealth as Factors in the Rise of Humanistic Thought," *Speculum*, XIII (1938), 1–37.

————. "Towards a More Positive Evaluation of the Fifteenth-Century Renaissance," *Journal of the History of Ideas*, IV (1943), 21–49.

BARRACCO, HELDA BULLOTTA. "Saggio bio-bibliografico su Enrico Cornelio Agrippa di Nettesheim," in Rome: Università. Instituto di filosofia. *Rassegna di filosofia*, VI, 3 (Luglio-settembre, 1957), 222–48.

BART, B. F. "Aspects of the Comic in Pulci and Rabelais," *MLQ*, XI (1950), 156–63.

BATIFFOL, LOUIS. *The Century of the Renaissance*, trans. Elsie Finnimore Buckley. New York, Putnam, 1916.

BAUDRIER, JULIEN. *Bibliographie lyonnaise. Recherches sur les imprimeurs, libraires, relieurs et fondeurs de lettres au XVIᵉ siècle*. Lyon-Paris, Brun, 1895–1921. 12 vols.

BAUR, ALBERT. *Maurice Scève et la renaissance lyonnaise*. Paris, Champion, 1906.

BAYON, H. P. "Calvin, Serveto and Rabelais," *Isis* (1948), 22–28.

BÉGUIN, SYLVIE. *L'Ecole de Fontainebleau*. Paris, Gonthier-Seghers, 1960.

BIRCH-HIRSCHFELD, ADOLF. *Das Fünfte buch des Pantagruel und sein verhältnis zu den authentischen büchern des romans*. Leipzig, Edelmann, 1901.

BLASER, ROBERT HENRI. *Paracelse et la conception de la nature. Travaux d'humanisme et renaissance*, III. Genève, Droz, 1950.

BLAU, JOSEPH L. *The Christian Interpretation of the Cabala in the Renaissance*. New York, Columbia University Press, 1944.

———. "Review of Egidio da Viterbo, *Libellus de litteris hebraicis: Scechina*, ed. F. Secret," *Renaissance News*, XIV (1961), 263–66.

BLOCH, ALEX. *Le Carré Magique SATOR. Collection Initiatique Illustrée*. Paris, Editions de F.E.U., 1963.

BLUNT, ANTHONY. *Art and Architecture in France, 1520–1700*. London-Baltimore, Penguin, 1953.

———. "The *Hypnerotomachia Poliphili* in 17th Century France," *Journal of the Warburg and Courtauld Institutes*, I (1937–38), 117–37.

———. *Philibert de l'Orme*. London, Zwemmer, 1958.

BOAS, GEORGE. *Essays on Primitivism and Related Ideas in the Middle Ages*. Baltimore, Johns Hopkins, 1948.

———. *Rationalism in Greek Philosophy*. Baltimore, Johns Hopkins, 1961.

BOLL, FRANZ JOHANNES, AND CARL BEZOLD. *Sternglaube und Sterndeutung, die geschichte und das wesen der astrologie*. Leipzig-Berlin, Teubner, 1926.

BORREN, CHARLES VAN DEN. "Rabelais et la musique," in Académie royale de Belgique. Classe des beaux arts. *Bulletin*, XXIV (1942), 78–111.

BOUCHÉ-LECLERCQ, AUGUSTE. *L'Astrologie grecque*. Paris, Leroux, 1899. 2 vols.

———. *Histoire de la divination dans l'antiquité*. Paris, Leroux, 1879. 4 vols.

BOUHIER, JEAN. "Remarques de Jean Bouhier sur les premiers 4 livres de Rabelais. . . ." B.N., Ms. fr., n.a. 4219.

BOULANGER, ANDRÉ. *Orphée: Rapports de l'orphisme et du chriſtianisme.* Paris, Rieder, 1925.

BOULENGER, JACQUES. "Notes sur la vie de Rabelais," *BHR,* I (1941), 30–42.

——. *Rabelais à travers les âges.* Paris, Le Divan, 1925.

——. "Le Vrai siècle de la Renaissance," *HR,* I (1934), 9–30.

BOUWSMA, WILLIAM J. *"Concordia Mundi": The Career and Thought of Guillaume Poſtel (1510–1581).* Cambridge, Mass., Harvard University Press, 1957.

BOWEN, WILLIS H. "Sixteenth Century French Translations of Machiavelli," *Italica,* XXVII (1950), 313–20.

BROWN, HUNTINGTON. *Rabelais in English Literature.* Cambridge, Mass., Harvard University Press, 1933.

BRUNET, JACQUES CHARLES. *Recherches bibliographiques et critiques sur les éditions originales des cinq livres du roman satirique de Rabelais. . . .* Paris, Potier, 1852.

BUSSON, HENRI. "Rabelaesiana: 'Science sans conscience,' (Pantagruel, VIII)," *HR,* VII (1940), 238–40.

——. "Rabelais et le miracle," *RCC,* XXX[1] (15 février 1929), 385–400.

——. *Les sources et le développement du rationalisme dans la littérature française de la renaissance (1533–1601).* Paris, Letouzey & Ané, 1922: revised as, *Le Rationalisme dans la littérature française de la renaissance (1533–1601).* Paris, Vrin, 1957.

CALDER, I. R. F. "A Note on Magic Squares in the Philosophy of Agrippa of Nettesheim," *Journal of the Warburg and Courtauld Inſtitutes,* XII (1949), 196–99.

CAMPROUX, CHARLES. "Du Pantagruélisme: à propos de la 'Couppe Testée' (En hommage à Abel Lefranc et à Leo Spitzer)," *Studi Francesi,* No. 16 (Gennaio-Aprile, 1962), 19–30.

CAROLUS-BARRÉ, LOUIS. "Le Contrat de mariage de Louis Le Caron. . . ," *BHR,* VII (1945), 252–57.

CARPENTER, NAN COOKE. "The Authenticity of Rabelais' Fifth Book: Musical Criteria," *MLQ,* XIII (1952), 299–305.

——. "Rabelais and the chanson," *PMLA,* LXV (1950), 212–32.

——. *Rabelais and Music.* Chapel Hill, N.C., University of North Carolina Press, 1954.

————. "Rabelais and Musical Ideas," *Romanic Review,* XLI (1950), 14–25.

CASELLA, MARIA TERESA. *Francesco Colonna, biografia e opere. Medioevo e umanesimo,* 1–2. Padua, Antenore, 1959.

CASSIRER, ERNST. *Das Erkenntnisproblem in der Philosophie und Wissenschaft der neuren Zeit.* Berlin, Cassirer, 1922. Vol. I.

————. "Giovanni Pico della Mirandola: A Study in the History of Renaissance Ideas," *Journal of the History of Ideas,* III (1942), 123–44, 319–46.

————. *The Individual and the Cosmos in Renaissance Philosophy,* trans. Mario Domandi. New York, Harper, 1964.

————. *Die Platonische Renaissance in England und die Schule von Cambridge.* Leipzig-Berlin, Teubner, 1932.

————. "Some Remarks on the Question of the Originality of the Renaissance," *Journal of the History of Ideas,* IV (1943), 49–56.

CASSIRER, ERNST, PAUL OSKAR KRISTELLER, AND JOHN HERMAN RANDALL, JR. *The Renaissance Philosophy of Man.* Chicago, University of Chicago Press, 1961.

CHAPPELL, ARTHUR F. "Rabelais and the Authority of the Ancients," *MLR,* XVIII (1923), 29–36.

CHASTEL, ANDRÉ. *Art et humanisme à Florence au temps de Laurent le Magnifique: Etudes sur la Renaissance et l'humanisme platonicien.* Paris, Presses Universitaires, 1959.

————. *Marsile Ficin et l'art. Travaux d'humanisme et renaissance,* XIV. Genève-Lille, Droz, 1954.

CHURCH, MARGARET. "The First English Pattern Poems," *PMLA,* LXI (1946), 636–50.

CHYDENIUS, JOHAN. "The Theory of Medieval Symbolism," in Societas Scientiarum Fennica, *Commentationes Humanarum Litterarum,* XXVII, 2 (1960), 42 pp.

CIRLOT, J. E. *A Dictionary of Symbols,* trans. Jack Sage. New York, Philosophical Library, 1962.

CLEMENT, NEMOURS HONORÉ. "A Note on Panurge," *Romanic Review,* XV (1924), 285–95.

————. *The Influence of the Arthurian Romances on the five Books of Rabelais.* Berkeley, Calif., University of California Press, 1926.

CLOUZOT, HENRI. "Philibert de l'Orme, Grand Architecte du roi mégiste (1548–1559)," *RSS,* IV (1916), 143–61.

COHEN, GUSTAVE. "Rabelais et le théâtre," *RER*, IX (1911), 1–72.

COUTAUD, ALBERT. *La pédagogie de Rabelais.* Paris, Librairie de la France scolaire, 1899. (B.N., R.15799).

DANIÉLOU, JEAN. *Platonisme et théologie mystique: Doctrine spirituelle de Saint Grégoire de Nysse.* Paris, Aubier, 1953.

DANNENFELDT, KARL H. "Egypt and Egyptian Antiquities in the Renaissance," *Studies in the Renaissance*, VI (1959), 7–27.

DELARUELLE, LOUIS. *Répertoire analytique et chronologique de la correspondance de Guillaume Budé.* Toulouse-Paris, Privat-Cornely, 1907.

DENOIX, L. "Les connaissances nautiques de Rabelais," in *François Rabelais: Ouvrage publié pour le quatrième centenaire de sa mort (1553–1953)*, Travaux d'humanisme et renaissance. Genève-Lille, Droz, 1953. Vol. VII, pp. 171–80.

DESGUINE, A. *Arcueil et les poètes du XVIᵉ siècle: La vigne, le vin et la tradition bachique à Arcueil-Cachan.* Paris, Champion, 1950.

DESTRÉE, CHARLES. "Une représentation du tournoi de la Quinte," *RSS*, X (1923), 224–25.

DIÈS, AUGUSTE. *Autour de Platon: Essais de critique et d'histoire.* Paris, Beauchesne, 1927.

DIGARD, ANICET. "Etudes sur les jurisconsultes du seizième siècle: Louis Le Caron, dit Charondas," *Revue historique de droit français et étranger*, VII (1861), 177–92.

DIMIER, LOUIS. *Histoire de la peinture française des origines au retour de Vouet: 1300–1627.* Paris-Bruxelles, Van Oest, 1925.

DROZ, EUGÉNIE. "Rabelais versificateur," *HR*, III (1936), 202–206.

DUBOUCHET, A. F. *Rabelais à Montpellier 1530–1538. Etude biographique d'après les documents originaux avec facsimile en héliogravures.* Montpellier, Coulet, 1887.

DUHEM, PIERRE. *Le Système du monde: Histoire des doctrines cosmologiques de Platon à Copernic.* Paris, Hermann, 1913–59. 9 vols.

DUPONT, A. "Note sur le quatrain de Nature Quite," *RSS*, XII (1925), 403–408.

EDELSTEIN, LUDWIG. "The Function of Myth in Plato's Philosophy," *Journal of the History of Ideas*, X (1949), 463–81.

EHRICHS, LUDWIG. *Les grandes et inestimables croniques de Gargantua und Rabelais "Gargantua et Pantagruel."* Strassburg, Trübner, 1889.

ELAUT, L. "Erasme, traducteur de Galien," *BHR*, XX (1958), 36–43.

ELDERKIN, GEORGE W. *Kantharos: Studies in Dionysiac and Kindred Cult.* Princeton, Princeton University Press, 1924.

EPHRUSSI, CHARLES. "Le Songe de Poliphile," *BBB* (1887), 305–38, 401–29, 457–77, 504–23.

ESKIN, STANLEY G. "Physis and Antiphysie: The Idea of Nature in Rabelais and Calcagnini," *Comparative Literature*, XIV (1962), 167–73.

FEBVRE, LUCIEN. *Autour de l'Hemptaméron: amour sacré, amour profane.* Paris, Gallimard, 1944.

———. *Le problème de l'incroyance au XVIᵉ siècle: La religion de Rabelais.* Paris, Michel, 1947.

FELLERER, KARL GUSTAV. "Agrippa von Nettesheim und die Musik," *Archiv für Musikwissenschaft*, XVI (Trossinger, 1959), 77–86.

FERGUSON, WALLACE KLIPPERT. *The Renaissance in Historical Thought.* Boston, Houghton-Mifflin, 1948.

FERRÈRE, F. "Erasme et le ciceronianisme au XVIᵉ siècle," *Revue de l'Agenais*, LI (1924), 176–82, 283–94, 342–57.

FESTUGIÈRE, A.-J. *Contemplation et vie contemplative selon Platon.* Paris, Vrin, 1950.

———. *Epicure et ses dieux.* Paris, 1946.

———. *La Philosophie de l'amour de Marsile Ficin et son influence sur la littérature française au XVIᵉ siècle. Etudes de philosophie médiévale,* XXXI. Paris, Vrin, 1941.

———. *La Révélation d'Hermès Trismégiste.* Paris, Gabalda, 1949–53. 4 vols.

FIERZ-DAVID, LINDA. *The Dream of Poliphilo, Related and Interpreted by Linda Fierz-David,* trans. Mary Hottinger. New York, Pantheon, 1950.

FRANCE, ANATOLE. *Rabelais.* Paris, Calmann-Lévy, 1928.

FRANCIS, K. H. "Rabelais and Mathematics," *BHR*, XXI (1959), 85–97.

François Rabelais: Ouvrage publié pour le quatrième centenaire de sa mort: 1553–1953. Travaux d'humanisme et renaissance. Genève-Lille, Droz, 1953. Vol. VII.

FRANÇON, MARCEL. *Autour de la lettre de Gargantua à son fils (Pantagruel, 8).* Rochecorbon, Gay, 1957.

———, ed. *Les croniques admirables du puissant roy Gargantua.* Rochecorbon, Gay, 1956.

———. "Note sur Rabelais et les nombres," *Isis*, XLI (1950), 298–300.

———. "Sur l'influence de Pétrarque en France au XVᵉ et au XVIᵉ siècles," *Italica*, XIX (1942), 105–10.

FRANTZEN, J.J.A.A. *Kritische Bemerkungen zu Fischarts Übersetzung von Rabelais' Gargantua.* Strassburg, Trübner, 1892.

FRIEDERICH, WERNER PAUL. *Dante's Fame Abroad, 1350–1850; the Influence of Dante Alighieri upon the Poets and Scholars of Spain, France, England, Germany, Switzerland and the United States.* Rome, Storia e letteratura, 1950.

GARIN, EUGENIO. *La Cultura filosofica del rinascimento italiano; ricerche e documenti.* Firenze, Sansoni, 1961.

———. *Giovanni Pico della Mirandola: Vita e dottrina.* Firenze, LeMonnier, 1937.

———. "Note sull' ermetismo del Rinascimento," in Rome: Instituto di Studi Filosofici, Archivio di Filosofia, *Testi Umanistici su l'Ermetismo* (1955), pp. 9–19.

GEBELIN, FRANÇOIS. *Les châteaux de la renaissance.* Paris, Les beaux arts, 1927.

GEBHART, EMILE. *Rabelais.* Paris, Lecène-Oudin, 1895.

———. *Rabelais, la renaissance et la réforme.* Paris, Hachette, 1877.

GILSON, ETIENNE. *History of Christian Philosophy in the Middle Ages.* New York, Random House, 1955.

———. "Notes médiévales au *Tiers Livre* de Pantagruel," *Revue d'Histoire franciscaine*, II (1925), 72–88.

———. "Rabelais franciscain," in *Les Idées et les lettres.* Paris, Vrin, 1932, pp. 197–241.

GLAUSER, ALFRED. *Rabelais créateur.* Paris, Nizet, 1966.

GOMBRICH, E. H. "Botticelli's Mythologies: A Study in the Neoplatonic Symbolism of his Circle," *Journal of the Warburg and Courtauld Institutes*, VIII (1945), 7–60.

———. "*Icones Symbolicae,* the Visual Image in Neo-Platonic Thought," *Journal of the Warburg and Courtauld Institutes,* XI (1948), 163–92.

GORDON, RICHARD. *F. Rabelais à la Faculté de médecine de Montpellier. Autographes et fac-simile. . . .* Montpellier, Coulet, 1876.

GRAD, A. D. *Pour comprendre la Kabbale.* Paris, Dervy-Livres, 1966.

GRAY, FLOYD. "Structure and Meaning in the Prologue to the *Tiers Livre,*" *L'Esprit créateur*, III, 2 (1963), 57–62.

GRÈVE, MARCEL DE. *L'Interprétation de Rabelais au XVIᵉ siècle. Etudes rabelaisiennes,* II. Genève, Droz, 1961.

GUARDINI, ROMANO. *Der Tod des Sokrates.* Godesberg, 1947.

GUITON, JEAN. "Le mythe des paroles gelées," *Romanic Review*, XXXI (1940), 3-15.

GUTMAN, HARRY B. "The Medieval Content of Raphael's 'School of Athens'," *Journal of the History of Ideas*, II (1941), 420-29.

HATZFELD, HELMUT. "Los Elementos constituyentes de la poesía mística," in *Actas del primer congreso internacional de hispanistas celebrado en Oxford del 6 al 17 de septiembre de 1962*, eds. Frank Pierce and Cyril A. Jones. Oxford, Dolphin, 1964.

HAUSER, HENRI, AND AUGUSTIN RENAUDET. *Les débuts de l'âge moderne. La renaissance et la réforme*. Paris, Alcan, 1938.

HAWKINS, RICHMOND L. "The *Querelle des amies*; the Platonism of Charles Fontaine," in *Maistre Charles Fontaine, parisien*. Cambridge, Mass., 1916, pp. 70-119.

HAYDN, HIRAM. *The Counter-Renaissance*. New York, Peter Smith, 1950.

HEINRICI, C. F. GEORG. *Die Hermes-Mystik und das Neue Testament*. Leipzig, Heinrichs, 1918.

HEULHARD, ARTHUR. *Rabelais: ses voyages en Italie, son exil à Metz*. Paris, Allison, 1891.

HORNIK, HENRY. "Jean-Antoine de Baïf's 'Les Presages d'Orpheus sur les tremblemens de terre': its significance, its source," *Studi Francesi*, No. 16 (Gennaio-Aprile, 1962), 81-83.

———. "Three Interpretations of the French Renaissance," *Studies in the Renaissance*, VII (1960), 43-66.

HUGUET, EDMOND EUGÈNE AUGUSTE. *Etude sur la syntaxe de Rabelais comparée à celle des autres prosateurs de 1450 à 1550*. Paris, Hachette, 1894.

HUIZINGA, JOHANN. *Homo ludens: A Study of the Play-Element in Culture*. Boston, Beacon, 1962.

HULUBEI, ALICE. "Virgile en France au XVIᵉ siècle: éditions, traductions, imitations," *RSS*, XVIII (1931), 1-77.

HUON, ANTOINETTE. "L'Alexandrinisme dans le *Quart Livre*," *Etudes rabelaisiennes*, I. Genève, Droz, 1956, pp. 98-111.

HUPPÉ, BERNARD F. *Doctrine and Poetry: Augustine's Influence on Old English Poetry*. Albany, New York, State University of New York Press, 1959.

HUTTON, JAMES. *The Greek Anthology in France and in the Latin Writers of the Netherlands to the Year 1800*. Ithaca, New York, Cornell University Press, 1946.

——. *The Greek Anthology in Italy to the Year 1800. Cornell Studies in English,* XXIII. Ithaca, New York, Cornell University Press, 1935.

IVANOFF, N. "La Beauté dans la philosophie de Marsile Ficin et de Léon Hébreux," *HR,* III (1936), 12–21.

JACOB, ERNST FRASER. *Cusanus the Theologian.* Manchester, Manchester University Press, 1937.

JANTZ, HAROLD STEIN. *Goethe's Faust as a Renaissance Man: Parallels and Prototypes.* Princeton, Princeton University Press, 1951.

JOURDA, PIERRE. *Le Gargantua de Rabelais.* Paris, Sfelt, 1948.

——. *Marguerite d'Angoulême, duchesse d'Alençon, reine de Navarre.* Paris, Champion, 1930. 2 vols.

JUNG, C. G. *Aion, Collected Works,* trans. R. F. C. Hull. New York, Pantheon, 1959. Vol. IX².

——. *Mysterium coniunctionis: An Inquiry into the Separation and Synthesis of Psychic Opposites in Alchemy, Collected Works,* trans. R. F. C. Hull, New York, Pantheon, 1963. Vol. XIV.

——. *Psychology and Alchemy, Collected Works,* trans. R. F. C. Hull. New York, Pantheon, 1953. Vol. XII.

——. *Psychology and Religion, Collected Works,* trans. R. F. C. Hull. New York, Pantheon, 1958. Vol. XI.

KAISER, WALTER JACOB. *Praisers of Folly: Erasmus, Rabelais, Shakespeare. Harvard Studies in Comparative Literature,* XXV. Cambridge, Mass., Harvard University Press, 1963.

KARPPE, S. *Etude sur les origines et la nature du 'Zóhar'.* Paris, Alcan, 1901.

KERR, W. A. R. "Le cercle d'amour," *PMLA,* XIX (1904), 33–63.

——. "The Pléiade and Platonism," *Modern Philology,* V (1907–08), 407–21.

KIBRE, PEARL. *The Library of Pico della Mirandola.* New York, Columbia University Press, 1936.

KLIBANSKY, RAYMOND. *The Continuity of the Platonic Tradition during the Middle Ages.* London, Warburg Institute, 1939.

KNIGHT, GARETH. *A Practical Guide to Qabalistic Symbolism.* New York, Helios, 1965. Vol. I.

KOYRÉ, ALEXANDRE. "Galileo and Plato," *Journal of the History of Ideas,* IV (1943), 400–28.

KRAILSHEIMER, A. J. *Rabelais and the Franciscans.* Oxford, Clarendon, 1963.

————. "Rabelais and the Pan Legend," *French Studies*, II (1948), 158–61.

————. "The Significance of the Pan Legend in Rabelais' Thought," *MLR*, LVI, 1 (1961), 13–23.

KRISTELLER, PAUL OSKAR. "Augustine and the Renaissance," *International Science*, I (1941), 7–14.

————. *Catalogus translationum et commentariorum: Mediaeval and Renaissance Latin Translations and Commentaries; annotated Lists and Guides.* Washington, Catholic University Press, 1960.

————. "Ficino and Pomponazzi on the Place of Man in the Universe," *Journal of the History of Ideas*, V (1944), 220–26.

————. *The Philosophy of Marsilio Ficino*, trans. Virginia Conant. New York, Columbia University Press, 1943.

————. *Renaissance Thought: The Classic, Scholastic, and Humanist Strains.* New York, Harper, 1961.

————. *Renaissance Thought II: Papers on Humanism and the Arts.* New York, Harper, 1965.

————. *Studies in Renaissance Thought and Letters. Storia e Letteratura*, LIV. Rome, Storia e Letteratura, 1956.

————. "Studies on Renaissance Humanism during the last Twenty Years," *Studies in the Renaissance*, IX (1962), 7–30.

————. *Supplementum Ficinianum.* Florentinae, 1937–45. 2 vols.

KRISTELLER, PAUL OSKAR, AND JOHN HERMAN RANDALL, JR. "The Studies of the Philosophies of the Renaissance," *Journal of the History Ideas*, II (1941), 449–96.

KUMMER, GÜNTER. *Das nachwirken der antiken komischen dichtung in den werken von Rabelais.* Berlin, Ebering, 1937.

LACROIX, PAUL. *Catalogue de la bibliothèque de l'abbaye de Saint Victor au seizième siècle, rédigé par François Rabelais.* . . . Paris, Techener, 1862.

LA JUILLIÈRE, PIERRE DE. *Les images dans Rabelais. Beihefte zur Zeitscheift für romanische Philologie*, XXXVII. Halle a.S., Niemeyer, 1912.

LANGLOIS, ERNEST. "Le Fumet du rôti payé au son de l'argent," *RER*, I (1903), 222–24.

LAPP, JOHN C. "Three Renaissance attitudes toward astrology: Rabelais, Montaigne and P. de Tyard," *PMLA*, LXIV (1949), 530–48.

LAUMONIER, PAUL. "L'Epitaphe de Rabelais par Ronsard," *RER*, I (1903), 205–16.

———. *Ronsard, poète lyrique: Etude historique et littéraire.* Paris, Hachette, 1909.

LEBÈGUE, RAYMOND. "Rabelais et la parodie," *BHR*, XIV (1952), 193–204.

———. "Rabelais, the Last of the Erasmians," *Journal of the Warburg Institute*, XII (1949), 91–100.

———. "La *République* de Platon et la Renaissance française," *Lettres d'Humanité*, II (1943), 141–65.

LECUYER, MAURICE A. *Balzac et Rabelais.* Paris, Société d'édition "Les Belles Lettres," 1956.

LE DOUBLE, A.-F. *Rabelais anatomiste et physiologiste.* Paris, Leroux, 1899.

LEFRANC, ABEL. "La civilisation intellectuelle en France à l'époque de la renaissance," *RCC*, XVIII[2] (1910), 58–68, 145–54, 721–39, 817–27; XIX[1] (1910–11), 49–60, 97–105, 145–54, 193–202, 241–49, 289–300, 337–45, 345–55, 433–53, 481–91, 529–39, 625–33, 673–82, 721–30, 769–77; XIX[2] (1911), 97–106, 145–54, 223–30, 289–96, 385–96, 481–91, 529–39, 673–83; XX (1911–12), 1–10, 49–58, 145–54, 289–301, 337–44, 500–09, 545–54.

———. *Le Collège de France (1530–1930) livre jubilaire composé à l'occasion de son quatrième centenaire.* Paris, Presses Universitaires, 1932.

———. *Grands écrivains français de la renaissance.* Paris, Champion, 1914.

———. *Les navigations de Pantagruel. Etude sur la géographie rabelaisienne. . . .* Paris, Leclerc, 1905.

———. "Notes pour le commentaire de Rabelais," *RER*, VII (1909), 433–39.

———. "Le Platon de Rabelais," *BBB*, (1901), 105–14, 169–81.

———. "Une poésie inconnue sur Rabelais (1538)," *RER*, I (1903), 202–203.

———. "Un prétendu V[e] livre de Rabelais," *RER*, I (1903), 29–54, 122–42.

———. "Rabelais et Cornélius Agrippa," *Mélanges offerts à M. Emile Picot* (Paris, Rahir, 1913), II, 477–86.

———. "Rabelais cité en 1547," *RER* (1905), III, 448.

———. *La Vie quotidienne au temps de la renaissance.* Paris, Hachette, 1938.

———. "Le vin chez Rabelais," *RSS*, XI (1924), 59–79.

LEGRAIN, GASTON. "Rabelais et les échecs," *RSS*, XV (1928), 151–55.

———. "Review of Jean Plattard, *Vie de François Rabelais*," *RSS*, XVI (1929), 166.

LESELLIER, J. "L'Absolution de Rabelais en cour de Rome: ses circonstances, ses résultats," *HR*, III (1936), 237–70.

———. "Deux enfants naturels de Rabelais légitimés par le Pape Paul III," *HR*, V (1938), 549–70.

LEWIS, DOMINIC BEVAN WYNDHAM. *Doctor Rabelais*, New York, Sheed and Ward, 1957.

LOVEJOY, ARTHUR O., AND GEORGE BOAS. *Primitivism and Related Ideas in Antiquity. A Documentary History of Primitivism and Related Ideas*, Vol. I. Baltimore, Johns Hopkins, 1935.

LOWINSKY, EDWARD. *Secret Chromatic Art in the Netherlands Motet*, trans. Carl Buchman. New York, Columbia University Press, 1946.

LUBAC, HENRI DE. *The Splendor of the Church*, trans. Michael Mason. New York, Sheed and Ward, 1956.

MARCEL, RAYMOND. *Marsile Ficin (1433–1499). Les Classiques de l'Humanisme*. Paris, Société d'édition "Les Belles Lettres," 1958.

MARGAROT, JEAN. "Rabelais médecin: La Médecine dans son oeuvre," *BHR*, XVI (1954), 25–40.

MARICHAL, ROBERT. "L'Attitude de Rabelais devant le Néoplatonisme et l'italianisme (*Quart Livre*, Ch. ix à xi)," in *François Rabelais: Ouvrage publié pour le quatrième centenaire de sa mort 1553–1953*. Travaux d'humanisme et renaissance. Genève-Lille, Droz, 1953. Vol. VII, pp. 181–209.

———. "Rabelais et la réforme de la justice," *BHR*, XIV (1952), 176–92.

MARTIN, VINCENT. "The Dialectical Process in the Philosophy of Nicholas of Cusa," *Laval théologique et philosophique*, V (1949), 213–68.

MARTIN-DUPONT, N. *François Rabelais*. Paris, Michel, 1910.

MASTERS, G. MALLARY. "The Hermetic and Platonic Tradition and Rabelais' *Dive Bouteille*," *Studi Francesi*, X (1966), 15–29.

———. "The Platonic and Hermetic Tradition and the *Cinquiesme Livre* of François Rabelais," unpublished doctoral dissertation, The Johns Hopkins University. Baltimore, 1964.

———. "Rabelais and Renaissance Figure Poems," *Etudes rabelaisiennes*, VIII, pp. 39–54.

MAURY, L.-F. Alfred. *La Magie et l'astrologie dans l'antiquité et au moyen âge*. Paris, Didier, 1877.

MÉRIGOT, LÉO. "Rabelais et l'alchimie," *Les Cahiers d'Hermès*, I (1947), 50–64.

MERLAN, PHILIP. *From Platonism to Neoplatonism.* The Hague, Nijhoff, 1960.

——. *Monopsychism, Mysticism, Metaconsciousness: Problems of the Soul in the Neoaristotelian and Neoplatonic Tradition.* Archives internationales d'histoire des idées, II. The Hague, Nijhoff, 1963.

MERRILL, ROBERT V., AND ROBERT J. CLEMENTS. *Platonism in French Renaissance Poetry.* New York, New York University Press, 1957.

METZKE, ERWIN. *Coincidentia oppositorum; Gesammelte Studien zur Philosophiegeschichte,* ed. Karlfried Gründer. Witten, Luther, 1961.

MEYLAN, EDWARD F. "L'évolution de la notion d'amour platonique," *HR,* V (1938), 418–42.

MILLET, RENÉ PHILIPPE. *Rabelais.* Paris, Hachette, 1892.

MÖNCH, WALTER. *Die italienische Platonrenaissance und ihre Bedeutung für Frankreichs Literatur und Geistesgeschichte (1450–1550).* Romanische Studien, XL. Berlin, Ebering, 1936.

MOULINIER, LOUIS. *Orphée et l'orphisme à l'époque classique.* Paris, Société d'édition "Les Belles Lettres," 1955.

MUSÉE CONDÉ À CHANTILLY. *Les très riches heures du Duc de Berry.* Paris, Nomis, 1949–50.

NARDI, ENZO. *Rabelais e il diritto romano.* Seminario giuridico della Università di Bologna, XXXIV. Milano, Giuffrè, 1962.

NAUDON, PAUL. *Rabelais franc-maçon. Essai sur la philosophie de Pantagruel.* Paris, La Balance, 1954.

NAUERT, CHARLES G., JR. *Agrippa and the Crisis of Renaissance Thought.* Illinois Studies in the Social Sciences, 55. Urbana, Ill., University of Illinois Press, 1965.

——. "Agrippa in Renaissance Italy: the Esoteric Tradition," *Studies in the Renaissance,* VI (1959), 195–222.

NICOLSON, MARJORIE HOPE. *The Breaking of the Circle.* New York, Columbia University Press, 1960.

NILSSON, MARTIN P. *The Dionysiac Mysteries of the Hellenistic and Roman Age.* Lund, Gleerup, 1957.

NOCK, ALBERT JAY, AND C. R. WILSON. *Francis Rabelais, the Man and his Work.* New York-London, Harper, 1929.

NOWOTONY, K. A. "The Construction of Certain Seals and Characters in the Work of Agrippa of Nettesheim," *Journal of the Warburg and Courtauld Institutes,* XII (1949), 46–57.

PAGEL, WALTER. *Paracelsus: An Introduction to Philosophical Medicine in the Era of the Renaissance.* Basel-New York, Karger, 1958.

PANOFSKY, DORA AND ERWIN. "The Iconography of the Galerie François Ier at Fontainebleau," *Gazette des Beaux-Arts,* ser. 6, LII (1958), 113-90.

PANOFSKY, ERWIN. *Studies in Iconology: Humanistic Themes in the Art of the Renaissance.* New York-Evanston, Harper, 1962.

PERRAT, CHARLES. "Autour du juge Bridoye: Rabelais et le *de Nobilitate* de Tiraqueau," *BHR,* XVI (1954), 41-57.

———. "Sur un tas de prognostications de Louvain," in *François Rabelais: Ouvrage publié pour le quatrième centenaire de sa mort,* pp. 60-73.

PERRIÈRE, J. DE LA. "Note pour le commentaire," *RER,* IV (1906), 264-67.

PEUCKERT, WILL-ERICH. *Pansophie: Ein Versuch zur Geschichte der weissen und schwarzen Magie.* Berlin, Erich Schmidt, 1956.

PICOT, EMILE. "Rabelais à l'entrevue d'Aiguesmortes (Juillet 1538)," *RER,* III (1905), 333-38.

PIERI, MARIUS. *Le pétrarquisme au XVIe siècle; Pétrarque et Ronsard, ou De l'influence de Pétrarque sur la Pléiade française.* Marseille, Lafitte, 1896.

PINVERT, LUCIEN. "Un entretien philosophique de Rabelais rapporté par Charondas (1556)," *RER,* I (1903), 193-201.

———. "Louis le Caron, dit Charondas (1536-1613)," *Revue de la Renaissance,* II (1902), 1-9, 69-76, 181-88.

PLAN, PIERRE PAUL. *Bibliographie rabelaisienne: Les éditions de Rabelais de 1532 à 1711.* Paris, Imprimerie nationale, 1904.

PLATTARD, JEAN. "L'Ecriture sainte et la littérature scriptuaire dans l'oeuvre de Rabelais," *RER,* VIII (1910), 257-330.

———. *Etat présent des études rabelaisiennes.* Paris, Société d'édition "Les Belles Lettres," 1927.

———. *François Rabelais.* Paris, Boivin, 1932.

———. *Guillaume Budé (1468-1540) et les origines de l'humanisme français.* Paris, Société d'édition "Les Belles Lettres," 1923.

———. *L'Invention et la composition dans l'oeuvre de Rabelais.* Paris, Champion, 1909.

———. *L'Œuvre de Rabelais (sources, invention et composition).* Paris, Champion, 1910.

———. "Les publications savantes de Rabelais," *RER,* II (1904), 67-77.

————. "Review of L. Sainéan, *Problèmes littéraires du xvie siècle,*" *RSS*, XIV (1927), 404–405.

————. *Vie de François Rabelais.* Paris-Bruxelles, Van Oest, 1928.

————. *La Vie et l'oeuvre de Rabelais.* Paris, Boivin, 1939.

PORCHER, JEAN. *Bibliothèque nationale, Paris, Rabelais; exposition organisée à l'occasion du quatrième centenaire de la publication de Pantagruel.* Editions des Bibliothèques nationales de France, 1933.

POWYS, JOHN COWPER. *Rabelais, his Life; the Story Told by him, Selections Therefrom Here Newly Translated, and an Interpretation of his Genius and his Religion.* New York, Philosophical Library, 1951.

PRÉCIGOU, ALPHONSE. *Rabelais et les limousins.* Limoges, Ducourtieux, 1906.

PROST, AUGUSTE. *Les Sciences et les arts occultes au XVIe siècle: Corneille Agrippa, sa vie et ses oeuvres.* Paris, Champion, 1881–82. 2 vols.

PUTNAM, SAMUEL. *François Rabelais, Man of the Renaissance, A Spiritual Biography.* New York, Cape & Smith, 1929.

RANDALL, J. H., JR. "The Development of Scientific Method in the School of Padua," *Journal of the History of Ideas*, I (1940), 177–206.

RANKE, LEOPOLD VON. *The ecclesiastical and political history of the Popes of Rome during the sixteenth and seventeenth centuries*, trans. Sarah Austin. Philadelphia, Lea and Blanchard, 1840–41. 5 vols.

REAUME, EUGÈNE. *Rabelais et Montaigne. Les idées de Rabelais et de Montaigne sur l'éducation* . . . Paris, Belin, 1888.

REITZENSTEIN, RICHARD. *Die Hellenistischen Mysterienreligionen.* Stuttgart, Teubner, 1956.

RENAUDET, AUGUSTIN. "Autour d'une définition de l'humanisme," *BHR*, VI (1945), 7–49.

————. *Etudes érasmiennes (1521–1529).* Paris, Droz, 1939.

————. *Humanisme et Renaissance; Dante, Pétrarque, Standonck, Erasme, Lefèvre d'Etaples, Marguerite de Navarre, Rabelais, Guichardin, Giordano Bruno.* Genève, Droz, 1958.

————. *Machiavel.* Paris, Gallimard, 1956.

————. *Préréforme et humanisme à Paris pendant les premières guerres d'Italie (1494–1517).* Paris, Champion, 1916.

REUSCH, FRANZ H. *Der Index der verbotenen Bücher, ein Beitrag zur Kirchen und Literaturgeschichte.* Bonn, Cohen, 1883–85.

————. *Die Indices librorum prohibitorum des sechzehnten Jahrhunderts.* Tübingen, Laupp, 1886.

ROE, FREDERICK CHARLES. *Sir Thomas Urquhart and Rabelais*. Oxford, Clarendon, 1957.

ROSSI, PAOLO. "The Legacy of Ramon Lull in Sixteenth-century Thought," *Medieval and Renaissance Studies*, V (1961), 182–213.

ROY, MAURICE. *Artistes et monuments de la renaissance en France*. Paris, Champion, 1929–34. 2 vols.

RÜEGG, WALTER. *Cicero and der Humanismus; formale Untersuchungen über Petrarca und Erasmus*. Zürich, Rheinverlag, 1946.

SAFRAN, ALEXANDRE. *La Cabale*. Paris, Payot, 1960.

SAINÉAN, LAZAR. "Le cinquième livre de Rabelais: son authenticité et ses parties constitutives," in *Problèmes littéraires du XVIe siècle*. Paris, Boccard, 1927.

————. "L'Histoire naturelle dans l'oeuvre de Rabelais," *RSS*, III (1915), 187–277; IV (1916), 36–104, 203–306; V (1917–18), 28–74; VI (1919), 84–113; VII (1920), 1–45, 185–205; VIII (1921), 1–41.

————. *L'Influence et la réputation de Rabelais; interprètes, lecteurs, et imitateurs*. . . . Paris, Gamber, 1930.

————. *La Langue de Rabelais*. Paris, Boccard 1922–23. 2 vols.

————. "Le Vocabulaire de Rabelais," *RER*, VI (1908), 285–316.

SALMON, GUILLAUME. *Dictionnaire hermétique*. Paris, d'Houry, 1695.

SALOMON, RICHARD. "A Trace of Dürer in Rabelais," *MLN*, LVIII (1943), 498–501.

SARTON, GEORGE. *The Appreciation of Ancient and Medieval Science during the Renaissance (1450–1600)*. Philadelphia, University of Pennsylvania Press, 1955.

————. "The Faith of a Humanist." Bruxelles, Weissenbruch, 1920.

————. *Galen of Pergamon*. Lawrence, Kansas, University of Kansas Press, 1954.

————. *Six Wings: Men of Science in the Renaissance*. Bloomington, Indiana, Indiana University Press, 1957.

SAULNIER, VERDUN L. *Le dessein de Rabelais*. Paris, Société d'édition d'enseignement supérieur, 1957.

————. "Dix années d'études sur Rabelais," *BHR*, XI (1949), 105–28.

————. "L'Enigme du Pantagruélion," *Etudes rabelaisiennes*, I, (Genève, 1956), 48–72.

————. "Etude sur Béroalde de Verville," *BHR*, V (1944), 209–326.

————. "François Rabelais, Patron des pronostiqueurs," *BHR*, XVI (1954), 124–38.

——. *Maurice Scève.* Paris, Klincksieck, 1948–49. 2 vols.

——. "Médecins de Montpellier au temps de Rabelais," *BHR*, XIX (1957), 425–79.

——. "Rabelais et le populaire," *Lettres d'Humanité*, VIII (1949), 149–79.

——. "Le Silence de Rabelais et le mythe des paroles gelées," in *François Rabelais: Ouvrage publié pour le quatrième centenaire de sa mort 1553–1953.* Travaux d'humanisme et renaissance. Genève-Lille, Droz, 1953. Vol. VII, pp. 233–47.

SCHMIDT, ALBERT-MARIE. "Haute science et poèmes français au XVIe siècle," *Cahiers d'Hermès*, I (1947), 11–49.

——. *Poésie scientifique en France au seizième siècle.* . . . Paris, Michel, 1940.

SCHNEIDER, WOLFGANG. *Lexikon Alchemistisch-Pharmazeutischer Symbole.* Weinheim, Chemie, 1962.

SCHOLEM, GERSHOM G. *Major Trends in Jewish Mysticism.* New York, Schocken, 1954.

——. *On the Kabbalah and Its Symbolism*, trans. Ralph Manheim. New York, University Books, 1965.

SCHRADER, LUDWIG. *Panurge und Hermes: Zum Ursprung eines Charakters bei Rabelais.* Bonn, Romanisches Seminar der Universität Bonn, 1958.

SCREECH, M. A. *L'Evangélisme de Rabelais: Aspects de la satire religieuse au XVIe siècle. Etudes rabelaisiennes*, II. Genève, Droz, 1959.

——. "An Interpretation of the *Querelle des Amyes*," *BHR*, XXI (1959), 103–30.

——. "The Meaning of Thaumaste," *BHR*, XXII (1960), 62–72.

——. *The Rabelaisian Marriage; Aspects of Rabelais's Religion, Ethics & Comic Philosophy.* London, Arnold, 1958.

SECRET, FRANÇOIS. "Jean Thénaud, voyageur et kabbaliste de la Renaissance, *BHR*, XVI (1954), 139–44.

——. "Les Jésuites et le kabbalisme chrétien à la renaissance," *BHR*, XX (1958), 542–55.

——. *Les Kabbalistes chrétiens de la Renaissance.* Paris, Dunod, 1964.

——. *Le Zóhar chez les Kabbalistes chrétiens de la Renaissance.* Paris, Durlacher, 1958.

SEIVER, GEORGE. "Cicero's *De Oratore* and Rabelais," *PMLA*, LIX (1944), 655–71.

SENEBIER, JEAN. *Catalogue raisonné de manuscrits conservés dans la Bibliothèque de la Ville & Republique de Genève.* Genève, Chirol, 1779.

SÉROUYA, HENRI. *La Kabbale, ses origines, sa psychologie mystique, sa métaphysique.* Paris, Grasset, 1957.

SEZNEC, JEAN. *The Survival of the Pagan Gods: The Mythological Tradition and its Place in Renaissance Humanism and Art,* trans. Barbara F. Sessions. New York, Harper, 1961.

SHOREY, PAUL. *Platonism, Ancient and Modern.* Berkeley, University of California Press, 1938.

SIMONE, FRANCO. *Il Rinascimento francese: studi e ricerche.* Torino, Società editrice internazionale, 1961.

SINGLETON, CHARLES S. *Journey to Beatrice, Dante Studies 2.* Cambridge, Mass., Harvard University Press, 1958.

SMITH, W. F. "On the Authenticity of the Fifth Book of Rabelais," *Modern Quarterly of Language and Literature,* I (1898–99), 283–89.

SÖLTOFT-JENSEN, H.-K. "Le Cinquième livre de Rabelais et le 'Songe de Poliphile,' " *RHLF,* III (1896), 608–12.

SPENCE, LEWIS. *An Encycolpaedia of Occultism.* New York, University Books, 1960.

SPITZER, LEO. *Classical and Christian Ideas of World Harmony: Prolegomena to an Interpretation of the Word 'Stimmung,'* ed. Anna Granville Hatcher. Baltimore, Johns Hopkins, 1963.

———. *A Method of Interpreting Literature.* Northampton, Mass., Smith College, 1949.

———. "Le prétendu réalisme de Rabelais," *Modern Philology,* XXXVII (1939–40), 139–50.

———. "Rabelais et les 'rabelaisants,' " *Studi Francesi,* IV (1960), 401–23.

———. *Die Wortbildung als stilistisches Mittel exemplifiziert an Rabelais* . . . Halle a.S., Niemeyer, 1910.

STAPFER, PAUL. *Rabelais sa personne, son génie, son oeuvre.* . . . Paris, Colin, 1896.

STAUB, HANS. "Scève, poète hermétique?" *Cahiers de l'Association internationale des études françaises,* XV (1963), 25–39.

STEINER, LEWIS H. *Paracelsus and his Influence on Chemistry and Medicine.* Chambersburg, Pa., Kieffer, 1853.

[STIRLING, WILLIAM.] *The Canon: An Exposition of the Pagan Mystery Perpetuated in the Cabala as the Rule of all the Arts.* London, Mathews, 1897.

TELLE, EMILE VILLEMEUR. *Erasme de Rotterdam et le septième sacrement; étude d'évangélisme matrimonial au XVI*° *siècle et contribution à la biographie intellectuelle d'Erasme.* Genève, Droz, 1954.

———. "L'Île des Alliances (Quart Livre, Chap. ix) ou l'Anti-Thélème," *BHR,* XIV (1952), 159–75.

———. *L'Œuvre de Marguerite d'Angoulême, reine de Navarre, et la Querelle des femmes.* Toulouse, Lion, 1937.

TETEL, MARCEL. "Aspects du comique dans les images de Rabelais," *L'Esprit créateur,* III, 2 (1963), 51–56.

———. *Etude sur le comique de Rabelais.* Florence, Olschki, 1964.

———. *Rabelais.* New York, Twayne, 1967.

THORNDIKE, LYNN. *A History of Magic and Experimental Science.* New York, Columbia University Press, 1923–41. 8 vols.

———. "The Place of Magic in the Intellectual History of Europe," *Studies in History, Economics and Public Law,* XXIV (New York, 1905), 1–110.

———. "Renaissance or Prerenaissance?" *Journal of the History of Ideas,* IV (1943), 65–74.

THUASNE, LOUIS. *Etudes sur Rabelais.* Paris, Bouillon, 1904.

———. *Villon et Rabelais; notes et commentaires.* Paris, Fischbacher, 1911.

TILLEY, ARTHUR. "The Authenticity of the Fifth Book of Rabelais," *Modern Quarterly of Language and Literature,* I (1898–99), 113–16.

———. *The Dawn of the French Renaissance.* Cambridge, Cambridge University Press, 1918.

———. *François Rabelais.* Philadelphia-London, Lippincott, 1907.

———. "The Literary Circle of Marguerite de Navarre," in *A Miscellany of Studies in Romance Languages and Literatures presented to Leo E. Kastner,* ed. Mary Williams & James A. de Rothschild. Cambridge, Cambridge University Press, 1932, pp. 518–31.

———. *Studies in the French Renaissance.* Cambridge, Cambridge University Press, 1922.

TOLDO, PIETRO. "Le Courtisan dans la littérature française et ses rapports avec l'oeuvre du Castiglione," *Archiv für das Studium der neuren Sprachen,* CIV (1899), 75–121, 313–30; CV (1900), 60–85.

———. "Encore la divination des signes," *RER,* II (1904), 40–43.

———. "La Fumée du rôti et la divination des signes," *RER,* I (1903), 13–28.

TRICOU, G. *Table de la Bibliographie lyonnaise du président Baudrier.* Genève-Lille, Droz, 1950.

UNDERHILL, EVELYN. *Mysticism: A Study in the Nature and Development of Man's Spiritual Consciousness.* New York, Dutton, 1961.

VILLEY-DESMESERETS, PIERRE LOUIS JOSEPH. *Marot et Rabelais avec une table chronologique des oeuvres de Marot,* in *Les grands écrivains du XVI⁰ siècle.* Paris, Champion, 1923.

VULLIAUD, PAUL. *La Kabbale juive.* Paris, Nourry, 1923.

WADDINGTON, CHARLES. *Ramus, sa vie, ses écrits et ses opinions (Paris, Meyrueis, 1855).* Dubuque, Iowa, Brown Reprint, 1962.

WAITE, ARTHUR EDWARD. *The Book of Ceremonial Magic.* New York, University Books, 1961.

————. *The Holy Kabbalah.* New York, University Books, 1960.

————. *Lives of Alchemystical Philosophers.* London, Redway, 1888.

————. *The Pictorial Key to the Tarot, Being Fragments of a Secret Tradition under the Veil of Divination.* New York, University Books, 1959.

————. *Studies in Mysticism and Certain Aspects of the Secret Tradition.* London, Hodder and Staughton, 1906.

WALKER, DANIEL P. "The Astral Body in Renaissance Medicine," *Journal of the Warburg and Courtauld Institutes,* XVI (1958), 119–33.

————. "Ficino's 'Spiritus' and music," *Annales Musicolog.,* I, (Paris, 1953), 131–50.

————. "Orpheus the Theologian and Renaissance Platonists," *Journal of the Warburg and Courtauld Institutes,* XVI (1953), 100–20.

————. "The *Prisca Theologia* in France," *Journal of the Warburg and Courtauld Institutes,* XVII (1954), 204–59.

————. *Spiritual and Demonic Magic from Ficino to Campanella.* London, Warburg Institute, 1958.

WELDMANN, KARL. *Der Einfluss der französischen auf Fischarts Wortschatz im Gargantua.* Giessen, 1913.

WEINBERG, FLORENCE MAY. "Rabelais and Christian Hermetism, the Wine and the Will," unpublished doctoral dissertation, the University of Rochester. Rochester, New York, 1967.

WHIBLEY, CHARLES. "Rabelais en Angleterre," *RER,* I (1903), 1–12.

WILAMOWITZ-MOELLENDORFF, ULRICH VON. *Die Textgeschichte der Griechischen Bukoliker.* Berlin, Weidmann, 1906.

WILKINS, ERNEST H. "A general survey of Renaissance petrarchism," *Comparative Literature,* II (1950), 327–42.

WILLIAMS, EDWARD B. "The Observation of Epistemon and Condign Punishment," *L'Esprit créateur,* III, 2 (1963), 63–67.

WILSON, HAROLD S. "Some Meanings of 'Nature' in Renaissance Literary Theory," *Journal of the History of Ideas,* II (1941), 430–48.

WIND, EDGAR. *Pagan Mysteries in the Renaissance.* New Haven, Yale University Press, 1958.

YATES, FRANCES A. *The French Academies of the Sixteenth Century.* London, Warburg Institute, 1947.

———. *Giordano Bruno and the Hermetic Tradition.* Chicago, 1964.

ZAMBELLI, C. "Testi Scelti di Cornelio Agrippa," in Rome: Instituto di Studi Filosofici, Archivio di Filosofia. *Testi Umanistici su l'Ermertismo* (1955), pp. 105–62.

ZANTA, LÉONTINE. *La Renaissance du stoicisme au XVI° siècle.* Paris, Champion, 1914.

ZELDIN, JESSE. "The Abbey and the Bottle," *L'Esprit créateur,* III, 2 (1963), 68–74.

INDEX

(The index contains names cited in the text and notes and major subjects listed primarily under the appropriate theme of Hermetism, Platonism, or the dialectic of opposites. Plato's dialogues are listed separately under his name and references to Rabelais's works appear at the end.)

ANALYTICAL REFERENCES TO RABELAIS